A Passion
to Lead!

A Passion to Lead!

How to Develop Your Natural Leadership Ability

Michael Plumstead

SkillPath Publications

Mission, KS

Project Editor: Kelly Scanlon

Editor: Jane Doyle Guthrie

Page Layout: Premila Malik Borchardt and Rod Hankins

Cover Design: Rod Hankins

ISBN: 1-57294-051-4

Library of Congress Catalog Card Number: 96-69147

10 9 8 7 6 5 4 3   06 07 08 09 10

Printed in the United States of America

Contents

Introduction

Leadership may be the most challenging interpersonal skill to develop. It is certainly the most complex. An orchestra conductor is leadership in action. Even when the conductor is at the most animated stage of conducting, there is a manic effortlessness. As an audience focuses on the conductor, the concert appears less complex. The conductor becomes the centerpiece, so we may miss the intensity of individual musicians.

It's a marvel to listen to such diverse instruments work in harmony. Each instrument has a different personality. The musicians who play often mirror the personality of the instrument. Trumpet players are sometimes brassy. Percussionists are perhaps a bit eccentric. Violinists have a studied grace. Certainly, these are stereotypes.

As we watch and listen to a concert, we are scarcely aware of the sacrifices that occurred before the concert. There were hours of practice. Strings practiced together. Brass practiced together. The entire orchestra practiced together. Perhaps there were arguments over seemingly minor details, such as how long the woodwinds hold a note before another instrument section starts a movement. The orchestra leader may have to deal with new performers, and worry over the funding of the orchestra.

We can make the same analogy using a stage play, a movie, or a sporting event. All of these events have talented people, led by a person who has to subvert his or her ego to the mission of the event. Perhaps that leader is a manager, coach, or director, or perhaps an actor or athlete whose professionalism and shining example are the foundation for success.

Leaders must have an intense desire to lead. One cannot lead without passion. One cannot lead without the willingness to make personal sacrifices for the mission and the people they lead. Great leaders set positive examples. Great leaders ask themselves how they may become more effective at their craft.

Reading this book will not make you a great leader. It will show you the most basic personal characteristics of great leaders. It will show you how to develop these characteristics. It will present exercises that will force you to ask yourself some difficult questions. That is one of the things great leaders learn early. They know that they must ask themselves hard questions before they earn the right to ask others to follow them.

This book will walk you through the important steps of leadership. You will learn some techniques for becoming a more effective leader. When you have completed the reading and exercises, you won't quite be ready to lead a large corporation. You will, however, have an idea of what it takes to lead a large corporation, or what it takes to lead a club or organization. Practice, and lots of it, will make you a great leader.

Part 1

Leadership Characteristics

Chapter 1

Leadership Defined

*T**he mist rose in the early morning, revealing two thousand soldiers prepared to follow your first command of battle. In the distance, a muted drum roll and the clink of steel against steel announce the approach of the enemy to the battlefield. Four thousand eyes gaze with confidence at the leader who has brought them to this great battle—you! You know it's yours to win …***

Most of us have fantasized at one time or another about leading an army into battle or a company into the top ranks of our profession. Many of us have dreamed about leading a sports team to a championship. As children, we may have imagined becoming a super hero, freeing the universe from the tyranny of villains and despots.

We live in a world that has spawned extraordinary leaders in recent history. The twentieth century has produced memorable figures like the Roosevelts, Golda Meier, John F. Kennedy, Nelson Mandela, Mother Teresa—all of them were very different people who used different aspects of their personality to lead. Some donned the cloak of leadership reluctantly, and led by great humility and personal sacrifice. Others sought the challenge of leadership for the glory it would bring to them. Some led quietly by example. Others were electric and inspiring. A few could lead in whatever fashion the situation dictated. Some led in the arts, others in science and technology. All, though, had a vision of their goals and the ability to communicate this vision to their constituencies. All had a great integrity in the principles they espoused. All had compassion for the people they led.

Some people think that leadership is about "being in charge" or "being the boss." There may even be a few anachronistic individuals who think being in charge means a relief from responsibility. You don't see the feet-on-the-desk, "where's my coffee?" type of boss much anymore. In fact, the term *boss* may imply domination and arrogance. It's a word that often conjures mistrust. There are, however, those who still believe that a leadership position is easier than being in the trenches. Teddy Roosevelt said it well when he stated, "The leader works in the open and the boss is covert. . . . The leader leads and the boss drives."

There *is* a difference between leadership and management. Management is the organization of tasks within a mission, goal, or objective that enables those in responsible positions to lead. Leadership suggests strong and direct interaction between the leader and those he or she leads. Good managers aren't necessarily good leaders. Strong leaders aren't necessarily good managers. The effective leader works to improve management skills. The efficient manager may have to work on interactive and personal skills.

At its core, to lead is to serve. Biographers write about how presidents, military leaders, and monarchs served their countries, served their people, and served their cause. A leader usually must answer to at least two constituencies. A military leader, for example, has a commanding officer plus soldiers under his or her care. The responsibility of leadership here is to obtain an objective with the fewest number of casualties.

That's not too different from the business world. A leader serves a corporation, the people who comprise the corporation, and the consumers who buy the corporation's products or services. That business leader's major responsibility is to make a profit, thus minimizing the personnel and monetary "casualties" that may arise from a river of red ink.

Leadership is not derived from power—power is derived from leadership. Having authority does not make one a leader. In the military, a freshly minted second lieutenant has authority. The noncommissioned officers (sergeants, corporals, etc.) with leadership experience have the power. The recent graduate of a corporate management training program may have the authority to sign checks or make work schedules, but line supervisors wield the power.

Leadership has to do with who you are—not what you do. Consistency in thinking leads to consistency in action. Those we lead trust us if we are true to strong personal values. Trust is an important pillar of any relationship. It is certainly the most important building block of leadership, as people will not follow a leader they cannot trust.

Leadership is not for those who can't follow. Leadership is not for those who place self-empowerment before empowerment of their constituency. Leadership does not wear well with those unaccustomed to personal sacrifice. For a leader, few things can replace the fire and confidence in the eyes of a team freshly led to victory as they anticipate the next challenge.

In the chapters that follow, you will learn the primary and secondary characteristics of great leaders. As you read the material, ask how these characteristics apply to you. Leadership necessitates that you practice. Leadership requires you to stretch your talent and your intelligence. Leadership demands that you grow.

Chapter 2

Primary Leadership Characteristics

Good leaders are good followers; they don't start life by being leaders. Certainly many may recall fellow students who were president of everything and captain of several sports teams, but those are the exceptions. It may be interesting to see the journey of some of them twenty years after their success. Many such achievers peak early if they don't learn to persevere, and if they don't truly believe leadership is their due.

You may have begun a foundation for leadership as a child or teen. Perhaps you were a member of a sports team, church group, Boy Scouts, Girl Scouts, 4H, or Junior Achievement. Maybe you sought office in high school or college in a fraternity, sorority, or student government. These are all experiences that may have taught you to follow a principle or an ideal. Think about some of the ideals you may have learned in these organizations. How do they apply to a current leadership situation?

Leaders surface in many areas of society besides business and government. Social and service organizations, church groups, and families require leaders too. Leaders are made, not born. Many people consider leadership an art. Remember that art is as much discipline as it is talent. Great artists discuss the "discipline" of their art as much as they discuss their talent and innovative techniques.

All of our heroes from history served an apprenticeship in *following*. Military greats first struggled at one of the service academies or in basic training, learning the craft of following. For some of them, the process of following was painful and filled with failure. Ulysses Grant finished near the bottom of his West Point class and failed at other occupations before becoming a successful commander during the Civil War.

Great business leaders often began their careers on the bottom rung, taking menial positions that helped them achieve their goals. Horatio Alger's late nineteenth-century books about young men who lived lives of virtue and overcame enormous obstacles fueled the imaginations of many business leaders of the twentieth century. In today's business world, many corporations have management training programs that teach the essentials of following. Trainees frequently work long hours performing entry-level or repetitive tasks. This course teaches them the basics of the career they have chosen and also tests their mettle—the good followers survive, and the mediocre look for other employment.

Powerful political leaders don't often begin their careers in the spotlight; more likely, they start out stuffing envelopes for a political mentor. In the process of following, they develop their visions, objectives, and styles. Harry Truman demonstrated his leadership capability as a young Army officer during World War I. He failed at everything else in his professional life until he entered politics. Truman continually confounded the political seers by following his vision and winning elections in spite of negative polls. Abraham Lincoln labored as an obscure regional politician. Though elected to Congress as a representative from Illinois, the newspapers of the day gave him scant notice until he won the presidency.

Of the many essential characteristics of great leaders to be discussed throughout the chapters that follow, the first step is the *desire to lead*. The origin of that motivation may be fame, fortune, cause, or change, but unless one has the desire to lead, the mission will fail. Good leaders will always examine and reaffirm why they want this responsibility. Great leaders may refrain from leading unless they feel a passion for leadership, knowing that the passion they radiate is often what their constituency follows.

If you believe you have a desire to lead, spend a few minutes with the following exercise.

Exercise #1:
Testing Your Leadership Mettle

- Consider the mission you are about to lead or a project you would like to head up (business, church, home, or school). In twenty-five words or less, jot down what you want to accomplish and why:

  _____

  _____

  _____

  _____

  _____

  _____

- List at least three ways you would communicate this objective to the people you want to lead:

  1. _____

  _____

  _____

  2. _____

  _____

  _____

  3. _____

  _____

  _____

Others:

_____

_____

_____

_____

_____

_____

_____

_____

- Imagine for a moment unlimited resources are at your disposal to accomplish your mission—whatever money you need is yours, and the people you require are available. There's a catch, though. You have to compromise the one quality in yourself you hold the dearest. Perhaps by compromising this quality, you will save several lives. What is that quality you value in yourself? Why would you compromise or not compromise this quality?

_____

_____

_____

_____

_____

_____

_____

_____

- Think for a moment about the people who will help you accomplish this mission. Imagine that you have one very qualified individual whose performance has been somewhat erratic. It may have been a long time since he or she contributed anything significant. Perhaps others within your group or organization have complained about him or her. You need to make a quick decision on this person to ensure the successful outcome of the mission. What would you do?

_____

_____

_____

_____

_____

_____

_____

_____

_____

_____

"V" Is for VICtory

Whatever outcome you may plan in your leadership quest, victory is what every leader seeks. Whether it's triumphing over evil, beating the competition, or winning on the playing field, victory is what you visualize. And where do you look for the essential ingredients of victory? Right in the first syllable: V-I-C. When you consider the many qualities that great leaders share, **V**ision, **I**ntegrity, and **C**ompassion are the key trio from which all the others spring. Courage springs from vision. Trust derives from integrity. Loyalty has its foundation in compassion.

One's level of vision, integrity, and compassion may determine the effectiveness of a leader. Although his adversaries criticized Abraham Lincoln's rusticity and crudeness, VIC was on his side during the Civil War. George Patton was bombastic and autocratic, but no one would deny he had vision, integrity, and compassion. He led his people mercilessly but cared for them deeply. Margaret Thatcher may have projected an icy aloofness, but who served as British prime minister longer than anyone in British history? Vision? Integrity? Compassion? You bet she had them!

Let's take a look at each one in greater detail.

Vision

Effective leaders have a clear vision of their objectives and how to get there. Most importantly, they're able to communicate this to their constituency. Leaders are "big picture" thinkers. While a manager may look at the individual building blocks of a project, a leader envisions the completed building and the relationship the individual bricks and mortar have to the whole project. Leaders are imaginative in this respect—they see what others do not. In the quest of their dream, they always see the glass as half full. They are dreamers, but with the knack of getting others to buy in to their dreams and participate. And their dreams are grounded in reality: leaders plan and set objectives and establish deadlines for achieving these objectives.

Great leaders may communicate in different ways. They may be terrific listeners with the gift of picking out the important content in a team member's conversation and using it to foster growth. They may communicate eloquently and passionately, glowing with the fire that burns within. They may be humorous—humor always lightens any burden. Some leaders don't appear to lead at all. Their approach is so low-key it leaves competitors scratching their heads in bewilderment. What's significant is the underlying transfer of the vision to the team.

Visualization is easy. Just imagine your goal or project completed to your satisfaction. Organize the elements to get it there, and communicate it to the people you lead. Don't be afraid to dream and share that dream with the people you lead! The next exercise offers a rudimentary map of the process.

Exercise #2:
Visualizing Your Dream to Reality

Take a few minutes to reflect on a project or a situation where you have a leadership role. In visualization, it helps to write down the details of your dream as the basis for a solid game plan.

- Compose a brief description of the situation as it currently exists:

_____

_____

_____

_____

_____

_____

_____

_____

_____

_____

_____

- Now write a brief description of the situation as you would like to see it:

  _____

  _____

  _____

  _____

  _____

  _____

  _____

  _____

- Jot down at least five needs you have to make the situation match your dreams:

  1. _____

     _____

  2. _____

     _____

  3. _____

     _____

  4. _____

     _____

  5. _____

     _____

Others:

_____

_____

_____

_____

_____

_____

- Construct a brief game plan for communicating these needs to the people you lead and to your immediate supervisor:

_____

_____

_____

_____

_____

_____

_____

_____

_____

_____

_____

Integrity

Integrity cuts deepest to an individual's character. An individual's degree of integrity *is* his or her character. The principles you hold dear and how you uphold them will determine how much trust your constituency will have in you. Margaret Thatcher became the dominant political figure in peacetime England in this century in large part because of her adherence to traditional British principles. She led the recovery of her nation by setting an example of what had made it a great nation to begin with. Her integrity was a large contributor to her rise to power in the conservative Party. She earned the sometimes grudging trust of fellow party members who were different than her in gender and social class. Her espousal of principle never wavered or changed during three terms as the prime minister. And it earned her the broad trust of friends and foe alike.

Integrity involves sticking to the "unvarnished truth" regardless of the consequences. It's adhering to the principle of "I cannot tell a lie." Integrity means making restitution for wrongs even though no one asks for restitution. Integrity is honesty and fair play in all of your business dealings. It's taking that extra stroke in a golf game when you're not sure.

In 1794 Thomas Paine stated: "It is necessary for the happiness of man that he be mentally faithful to himself. Infidelity does not consist of believing or disbelieving; it consists of professing to believe in what one does not believe." If you have ever walked away with your head held high from an incident that would compromise your principles, you know what Paine was saying. If you can look your mirror reflection in the eye each night, knowing you've done your best, you can look those you lead in the eye and not compromise the principles you hold dear. Developing this ability and protecting this standard communicates your vision to those you lead better than anything else you can do. Living and communicating integrity is vital for setting the example of leadership. The following exercise examines the concept more personally.

Exercise #3:
Developing Integrity

- Name three people in your personal or professional life who embody the characteristics of integrity and don't compromise ideals:

  1. _____
  2. _____
  3. _____

- List a reason why you feel each person has this trait:

Person #1. _____

_____

_____

_____

Person #2. _____

_____

_____

_____

Person #3. _____

_____

_____

_____

- Identify what you can learn from these people and apply to your role as a leader:

Person #1. _____

_____

_____

_____

_____

Person #2. _____

_____

_____

_____

_____

Person #3. _____

_____

_____

_____

_____

Compassion

Respect for the people you lead and a conscious effort to contribute to their welfare are the benchmarks of compassionate leadership. In the military, this responsibility for the people you lead extends to their very survival. In whatever leadership situation you may find yourself, you are responsible for the "care and feeding" of those you lead. You are responsible for their professional survival. Although your constituency also has a responsibility, you often must guide them toward it.

As a leader, you are in many cases responsible for your team's emotional survival as well. Getting a faltering employee back on his or her feet emotionally is often part of the compassion demanded of leadership. There's nothing more rewarding for a leader than successfully redirecting the efforts of a team member in a slump. Such action also has a side benefit: Other team members recognize compassionate acts, and these deeds inspire better performance in everyone. Note that this does not mean abandoning the mission for the sake of one individual—a good leader needs to recognize when compassion endangers the success or welfare of other employees or team members. It's difficult to lead people who are self-absorbed or despairing, and they can undermine an entire project or process. Compassion in these circumstances would suggest removing such individuals from the mission.

The compassionate leader is by necessity an introspective one. Compassionate leadership demands first looking to your own style or contribution when things go amiss. Introspection heightens your responsibility and builds trust in those who must accomplish a mission with you.

The compassionate leader exercises all options before issuing reprimands or discharging personnel. He or she recognizes that creating fear in constituents creates stress and reduces production immeasurably over a long time. Followers who are afraid of their leaders concentrate on finding an escape route. Individuals who use fear as their primary means of leadership usually find themselves facing the trials of the marketplace alone. Complete the next exercise to get a closer look at the trait of compassion.

Exercise #4:
Developing Your Compassionate Side

- Would the people you lead consider you a compassionate person? Why?

  _____

  _____

  _____

  _____

  _____

- When was the last time you demonstrated compassion to those you lead—where you did something that was truly uplifting to them?

  _____

  _____

  _____

  _____

  _____

  _____

- Take a moment to think about at least three key people in your personal, social, or professional life who look to you for leadership. Write down how you may show them compassion if you're not already doing so:

Person #1. _____

_____

_____

_____

_____

Person #2. _____

_____

_____

_____

_____

Person #3. _____

_____

_____

_____

_____

Chapter 3

Secondary Leadership Characteristics

The secondary characteristics of leadership have as much to do with how a leader communicates as they do with the leader's actual personal traits. The communication of leadership is much more than the ability to stand in front of your army and exhort the troops to victory. If a leader gives a speech that is dazzling in its motivational impact but then walks away and allows the mission to run its course, he or she is sending the wrong message. That mission will not succeed. A leader communicates best by the example he or she sets.

Many of the examples General Robert E. Lee set in his life communicated a much more powerful message than anything he ever said. One of these relates to his attendance at an Episcopalian church in Richmond after the Civil War. When it came time for communion, a former slave made his way to the altar railing and knelt to receive. A shocked hush fell over the open-mouthed congregation. The only sound in the church was that of solitary footsteps, as the resolute, gray image of Robert E. Lee walked down the aisle. He knelt by the side of the former slave to receive communion.

The following questionnaire will help you determine if you possess the ten secondary leadership characteristics that flow from **V**ision, **I**ntegrity, and **C**ompassion.

Exercise #5:
Which Leadership Characteristics Do You Possess?

Place a check mark in the appropriate box in response to each statement.

	Yes	Sometimes	No
1. I can make decisions without being concerned with what others think.	☐	☐	☐
2. As a manager or within my circle of friends, I am the first to suggest a course of action.	☐	☐	☐
3. I can project enthusiasm even when I do not feel enthusiastic.	☐	☐	☐
4. I usually feel a high level of energy when I'm involved in projects I like.	☐	☐	☐
5. When I'm faced with an obstacle in the pursuit of an objective, I will try several times to remove or avoid the obstacle before I abandon the objective.	☐	☐	☐
6. People think that flexibility is one of my strongest characteristics.	☐	☐	☐

	Yes	Sometimes	No
7. I exhibit more self-confidence than most people I encounter.	☐	☐	☐
8. People tell me I have a creative or inventive mind.	☐	☐	☐
9. I attend a seminar or read a book related to my professional skills at least every six months.	☐	☐	☐
10. I always make objective decisions.	☐	☐	☐
11. Friends or business associates have complimented me on my good judgment.	☐	☐	☐

If you answered "no" to three or more of these statements, you will need to make a concentrated effort to develop your leadership potential, but don't be discouraged. Leaders all have weaknesses to overcome. For example, not everyone may have a creative or inventive mind—a characteristic that can be difficult to develop. Consequently, you could work to develop your own creativity, or you could hire creative people as advisors.

If you responded "sometimes" to any of the eleven statements, these are areas that need polish or improvement. Even if you replied "yes" to each statement, there are always things a leader can improve. Let's examine these secondary leadership characteristics in further detail in order understand them better.

Courage

Courage is not freedom from fear—it's actually the ability to *use* fear to obtain your objectives. Fear generates much energy. All good actors get "stage fright" before a performance, regardless of their experience. That "stage fright" is due to a fear of the audience "not liking me." Even experienced actors become terrified over forgetting their lines in a key scene. Leaders are on stage too and have the same desire to give the performance of their lives. Just as actors do, successful leaders learn to visualize a successful outcome. They begin to harness the energy of fear to give courageous performances. Courage flows from vision and integrity. When you believe in your vision and are true to your values, you will have courage. To illustrate, think about a time in your life when you knew you were "really right." Did you not have less fear in expressing yourself?

Initiative

Initiative is a direct result of wanting to get the job done. This quality of "taking the bull by the horns" or "acting like an eager beaver" helps many people who have come up through the sales ranks become CEOs. Effective salespeople live by the axiom that "nothing happens until someone sells something." Remember that selling is often a process of removing obstacles that demotivate a potential buyer. If you're the type of person who has many suggestions for getting things done plus the plan to accomplish them, you have initiative. Of the ten secondary qualities of leadership, initiative is the most important. Unless you have the capacity to initiate action and follow up on execution, you will not be an effective or well-respected leader.

Initiative also means taking responsibility for the consequences of your initiatives. If an idea or play you implement causes professional or personal casualties, you may find yourself leading in an empty room!

Enthusiasm

Enthusiasm flows from what we hold inside ourselves. Many people have enthusiasm but don't know how to project it; they're afraid of looking foolish if they appear to be having too much fun in their leadership role. Often, enthusiasm will carry the day over experience. The sports pages, for example, frequently show examples of young, *enthusiastic* sports teams upsetting experienced rivals. This points to a leader—a veteran player on the team or a manager or coach—who was obviously enthusiastic about the mission and able to communicate this to the players. Enthusiasm sells when all else fails. A leader has to constantly sell team members on the idea of victory and achievement. When a team reflects the enthusiasm of its leader, the members don't have time to think about failure. Practice enthusiasm and you will feel it.

Energy

Energy is a characteristic that is often generated by a person's belief in his or her mission. The passion an individual has for the mission of leadership often becomes the fuel for success. Radiating energy is a positive form of communication. It creates momentum.

Leadership requires stamina. By definition, leaders have to lead from *in front* of their people. They are "on stage" for all to see. Their actions are the benchmark everyone else strives for. It's necessary then for leaders to project energy and endurance. A leader who projects fatigue may find constituents waiting for the chance to take a nap themselves.

In the military, physical fitness represents a critical part of a leader's efficiency report, but it's just as important for a business leader to maintain an appropriate level of physical fitness too. A leader who doesn't won't have the energy and stamina the job requires. Scientists and doctors are learning more every day about how diet and exercise can affect our energy level. Of the 168 hours available in a week, spend three or four on an exercise program. Remember, it requires energy to be out in front.

Perseverance

Perseverance often means never quitting, but prudence should temper this approach. Leaders can never allow perseverance to become stubbornness or intractability. Those with a clear vision of their objectives are more able to persevere than those who lack such a picture. They are able to persevere because they have committed their vision to a carefully scripted battle plan that allows them to anticipate bumps in the road. Perseverance shows commitment, which in turn always sends a positive message to the people one leads. "Winners never quit and quitters never win" is an old saying that appropriately describes the outcome for those who persevere.

Flexibility

Flexibility is not the same as vacillation. Good quarterbacks who have practiced their game plan can confidently call "audibles" at the line of scrimmage when a situation changes. A good game plan allows a leader to zig and zag when necessary.

Flexibility also entails being approachable. It's important to spend quality professional time with your team members at work to learn how they think and what contributions they can make to the team effort in an emergency. Being approachable also encourages team members to keep you apprised of situations that could derail a project or the course of your business. You might think of flexibility as "bending." Effective leaders learn to bend and stretch for the needs of their team. They also remember to bend *toward* their team members to hear what each has to say.

Self-Confidence

Without self-confidence, a leader can't survive. Those being led know when a leader has the right stuff. No one can "bluff" self-confidence for very long. Some people are raised in an environment that creates self-confidence. Others have survived emotional or physical pain to become stronger people who project self-confidence. If you don't feel self-confident, it's important to sit down with a pencil and sheet of paper and list your accomplishments. You'll be surprised at how many you have. Sometimes we lack confidence because we don't spend enough time thinking about the contributions we've made to others or ourselves. Never let imagined failures erode your self-confidence. Remember, though, that occasional real failure is a part of life. It's how you view these failures that determines the impact they'll have on your self-confidence. Try to view them as *practice* for achieving your goals.

Creativity

Creativity emerges in many ways. Perhaps you're the type of leader who can always see things differently than others. Maybe you're creative in how you praise people or tune in to all the different ways they can be motivated. Leaders who can turn the proverbial sow's ear into a silk purse are especially creative; perhaps you can do this by establishing a comfortable work environment for your people on a very limited budget. Creativity is a highly intangible quality and difficult to specifically define. When people speak of "inspired leadership," they are often actually referring to creativity, as in a magic moment when a leader performs a quick miracle that accelerates a project that's losing momentum. What about leaders who appear totally devoid of creativity but have a knack for hiring people with the qualities they lack? Is that creative? You bet!

Education

A leader's education doesn't necessarily occur through *formal* education. That is, although you may study leadership, achievement comes through actual practice. Effective leaders continually pick up pieces of knowledge. They study people and watch how they interact. They observe what motivates people.

Good leaders are also readers who learn all they can about their chosen profession and the conditions that change or modify their role. They aren't afraid of exposure to novel ideas. Because such leaders are introspective, they will commit to learning whatever may guide them to a more productive management style.

Productive leaders also educate themselves by always asking what they can learn from other people. They invite the opinions of others—of their advisors, their staff, and workers.

Just keep in mind that you must put what you learn into practice. Knowledge is power—but only if you act on it.

Objectivity

Objectivity is the ability to see both sides of an issue. Many times as a leader you will have to arbitrate disputes or negotiate goals and objectives; therefore, it's very important to present a balanced perspective to the people you lead. For example, imagine that a directive arrives from your higher authority that you feel makes your mission difficult or impossible to accomplish. Objectively, you have a responsibility to seek clarification and negotiate away the "mission killer" elements of the directive before you show a reaction to your constituency. This is an element of leadership that calls for crucial timing. Pick up monkey wrenches gingerly and discard them carefully. Resist the temptation to hurl them at plate glass windows! The best way to nurture objectivity is to count to ten before you act. Sit down and make a list of why an opposing viewpoint exists. Give strong consideration to what you can change and what you can't.

The source of most problems that tend to cloud our objectivity is *miscommunication*. Showing a lack of objectivity to your constituency will slow the mission down even more. You may have to take a step backward to clarify or redirect miscommunication, but that's better than jeopardizing or really delaying a mission by sending confusing messages to your team.

Judgment

Good judgment follows as a result of flexibility and objectivity—it's not a standalone characteristic. The introspective leader is always questioning his or her judgment relative to desired outcomes:

- Will my decisions make things more effective and more efficient?

- Is this decision fair to the people I lead?

- Is it fair to the people who have charged me with the responsibility of leadership?

Good judgment has little to do with how a decision affects "me" and more to do with how the decision affects "we." Good judgment is generous; it has a sense of fair play and may leave room for a vanquished opponent to retain some pride. Ulysses Grant demanded unconditional surrender of the Confederacy at Appomatax Courthouse, but he allowed the vanquished enemy to keep their horses and weapons to farm and hunt—a vivid example of good and compassionate judgment. The nation needed to be rebuilt, and allowing the defeated enemy to retain their horses and rifles enabled them to begin the process by first rebuilding their self-esteem.

Exercise #6:
Finding Ways to Improve Your Leadership Characteristics

- What are your three strongest secondary leadership characteristics?

    1. _____

    2. _____

    3. _____

- Give a brief summary of what you think you can do to make these characteristics stronger.

    Characteristic #1._____

    _____

    _____

    Characteristic #2._____

    _____

    _____

    Characteristic #3._____

    _____

    _____

- What are your three weakest secondary leadership characteristics?

    1. _____

    2. _____

    3. _____

- How could these weaknesses affect the team or project you lead?

Characteristic #1._____

    _____

    _____

    _____

Characteristic #2._____

    _____

    _____

    _____

Characteristic #3._____

    _____

    _____

    _____

• How can you eliminate these weaknesses (or at least minimize them)?

Characteristic #1. _____

_____

_____

_____

Characteristic #2. _____

_____

_____

_____

Characteristic #3. _____

_____

_____

_____

Part 2

Developing and Following Leadership Styles

Chapter 4

Leadership Styles

Your personality shapes your style of direct communication with others, which in turn both shapes and expresses your leadership style. If there were talented storytellers in your family, you may have a predisposition to use anecdotes effectively to make your point. If both your parents were mathematicians and talked about theory at the dinner table, you may have a love for data. A nurturing childhood with frequent family reunions may add an "extended family" flavor to your leadership style. Our early environment and even birth rank impacts the leaders we become—oldest children may be more conscious of setting an example. Middle kids can see both sides of an issue more readily. Youngest family members may constantly seek attention and applause.

Although genetics and child rearing are fields that obviously won't be explored too deeply in a book on leadership, it's important to realize that you play only a small part in shaping your personality until you become an adult. As you leave high school, your personality style is in rough form. If leadership is one of your goals, your basic leadership personality style will have been shaped by those first seventeen or eighteen years. The personality is "rough cut" and awaits the molding, planing, and finishing of life experience. We are all works in progress.

The most important aspect of communicating with others and shaping our personalities is *understanding ourselves*. Forceful leaders are effective communicators. You communicate your vision, integrity, and compassion by what you do as well as by what you say. In understanding and developing a leadership style, it's important to realize that what you do always speaks louder to your constituents than what you say. A leader who doesn't follow up on his or her message loses credibility. Empty promises cause followers to evaporate. Leaders who set a poor example will see team members drift away.

Leaders who set standards and then exceed them in their individual examples of self-discipline can expect the same in return. Some leaders are able to set very high standards for themselves and leave some latitude for their constituency. By individually coaching their team members, leaders can increase team members' self-confidence and help them to higher levels of achievement.

It's vitally important to have a clear vision of yourself if you're going to be a successful leader. Why? When you put on the "uniform" of leader, everyone else will pick up their microscopes and magnifying glasses. Want an illustration of this phenomenon? Pick up the newspaper today and see how many times national leaders are second-guessed. Even better, read the sports page for an analysis of what the coach *should* have done last night to win the game. Even if you're not a fan, the sports page can sometimes offer you a sharper insight into leadership and management than *The Wall Street Journal*. It's a daily chronicle of how leadership succeeded or failed.

Characteristically, leaders look at the forest and not the trees. Managers are usually tree watchers. Followers may each be a tree or have one of their own. In order for a follower to become a leader, he or she has to become a forest watcher. This doesn't mean second-guessing leaders; it means examining why they do the things they do and evaluating the results for future reference. In the process of this evaluation, the follower also takes stock of his or her own talents and inserts them in the parts of the mission where they can contribute the most. Of course, consultation and agreement with active leadership is a necessary step in this process.

"Big picture" thinking is a requirement of discerning leaders. Followers with leadership aspirations must become "big picture" followers. Remember that poor leaders were usually poor followers. You've seen poor followers—the ones who complain and never offer solutions. At their worst, they would rather see a mission derailed than make a suggestion for its success.

"Big picture" followers are able to exert internal leadership that keeps missions on track. They mentor new hires. They look for ways to parallel and complement the style of a leader who matches their own. Many people prefer to stay in this role of internal leader. Sales teams, for example, may have one high-producing representative who always outearns management. He or she may informally counsel others on everything from policy to technique. The perception often is that this "big picture" follower will have a more objective viewpoint than management. A leader may view this type of team member as a blessing if he or she sets a good example for other team members.

The next four chapters will describe four leadership styles. The self-test at the beginning of each chapter will help you determine if the focus style is your own. You'll benefit from taking all the tests. If you find yourself identifying with several characteristics from each style of leadership, that's good! This indicates a well-centered leadership personality, one that's crucial in relating to different people.

You'll also find "stretching exercises" at the end of each chapter. It's beneficial to use all of these exercises, even if you don't fall into the particular personality category the exercise covers. Completing the exercise will help you develop the introspection you need to be a powerful leader—you'll gain additional insight into how others think and what they need for growth.

As you learn about different leadership styles, don't forget to draw a distinction between *leadership* and *management*. Leadership is about who you are; management is about what you do.

Chapter 5

The Warrior

magine a well-sculpted Grecian figure poised to launch a spear. Your image may be one of cold marble or hard steel. Hooded eyes focus on an invisible target in the distance. Moving forward in time, the image changes to someone austerely but fashionably dressed. The armor is dark clothing with red accents—a tie or scarf. The posture is erect and commanding. Sound familiar? Respond to the statements in Exercise #7 to find out whether you model the Warrior style of leadership.

Exercise #7:
Recognizing the Warrior in You

	Yes	No
1. "Spare the details and get to the bottom line" sums up my attitude toward completing a project.	☐	☐
2. Showing too much emotion can set a bad example for the people I lead.	☐	☐
3. "I don't feel pressure, I create it" could be my favorite quip.	☐	☐
4. "Time is of the essence" could be one of my mottoes.	☐	☐
5. I have high expectations of myself and the people around me.	☐	☐
6. My associates consider me independent and ambitious.	☐	☐
7. On the way to an objective, I know I step on toes and sometimes hurt the feelings of co-workers.	☐	☐
8. When making decisions, I like options and probabilities.	☐	☐
9. I often interrupt the conversations of others.	☐	☐
10. I would rather my superiors support my conclusions than my feelings.	☐	☐

Responding "yes" to at least seven answers places you in the Warrior category of leadership.

Personality Snapshots

As you enter the office of a Warrior type, the wall decor reflects individual accomplishment. There may be certificates of achievement or military decorations. You probably won't see any pictures of the person shaking hands with celebrities. Family pictures may line up like a military formation on the credenza. Neat piles of projects in progress may cover the desktop.

The furniture in the office will be very functional and not very comfortable. You are belatedly offered coffee or a soft drink. The Warrior may appear distracted, as if poised for another mission.

As you engage this person in conversation, you'll notice minimal eye contact. He or she will always seem to be looking at some faraway spot on the wall behind you. When eye contact occurs, it will be very penetrating and very brief. It serves to make a strong point.

Body language may be open or closed, depending on the discussion. The Warrior has a tendency to lean forward in his or her chair and not use much hand gesturing. Any gestures the Warrior does use will be somewhat awkward and uncomfortable, much like the choppy gestures you see the late President Kennedy making during speeches in old news clips. They are the movements of a person who may have learned the importance of hand gestures when speaking in public but is uncomfortable using them.

Don't be surprised if the Warrior looks at a watch or a clock frequently. These people place a very high value on time. If conversation strays from the topic, you may hear, "What's the point?" or "Get to the point!" If you're making a presentation, expect questions like "What are my choices?" or "What's the bottom line?" from a Warrior—as well as frequent interruptions. Ask a Warrior what he or she thinks will happen in the future and you'll get a long, well-focused monologue, delivered while gazing at that distant horizon behind you.

The Warrior has a sense of humor but is not a storyteller. Among friends this humor often takes the form of rapier-sharp one-liners. Warriors also think festive occasions are fine as long as someone else does the planning

You probably know someone like the Warrior, even if you're not this way yourself. Warriors are strong on vision, and at their best have a great deal of integrity. Though compassionate, they don't always project this quality.

Challenge is the primary motivator for the Warrior. Trappings and privileges take a distant second, though a Warrior may accept them as a reward for a job well done.

Leadership roles attract this type of personality more than any of the others that will be discussed in this book.

Improving Leadership Skills

If you're a Warrior, detractors may refer to you as pushy, severe, tough-minded, dominating, or harsh; you would prefer to think of yourself as determined, thorough, decisive, and efficient. Often the truth lies somewhere in the middle. To be a more positive leader, you'll have to work the hardest on projecting compassion.

Those you lead may not consider you a good listener. Impatience may cause you to interrupt conversations, which discourages more sensitive team members with less assertive personalities than yours. They may perceive your brusqueness as intimidation and perhaps avoid you as a result. If you work with talented, worthwhile team members, it will pay you big dividends to spend some extra time listening to how their Aunt June won a blue ribbon for her "triple threat" jalapeno jelly. Schedule individual time with team members, either informally in your office or at their workstations. Loosen the stiff upper lip and let it sneak into a smile from time to time.

When you're under pressure, you may have a tendency to become more authoritarian. The hallway trembles as you stride from one end to the other. Doors slam and employees hide. Of course, perhaps that's what you want when you're pushing for results, but it doesn't work in the long run. The people you lead will lose trust in you if they feel they're being ignored or unnecessarily controlled. Your style is to control. When you're under pressure, you may tend to overcontrol and show impatience if things don't happen fast enough. This can be very demoralizing for your team members—other professionals accustomed to a certain amount of autonomy.

You may need to delegate some of the workload. If the leadership role is new to you, resist the temptation to handle everything alone. You may also fall into this trap when you're under pressure. "It's quicker and easier to do it myself" could be one of your mottoes. Although delegation is covered in a later chapter, it's important to point out here that this is an area where the Warrior type of leader usually needs some practice.

Unless you have come to your leadership position through sales, you may not be aware of your tendency toward poor eye contact. You make eye contact, of course, but it's usually fleeting and penetrating. When talking with people, try to focus on what they're saying and watch them when you talk to them. Good eye contact projects compassion and gives the people you're communicating with the sense that you care about what they're saying.

Because you may be blunt in your interactions, you may need to guard against appearing overly critical in your communication with those you lead. Learn to ask why they may have done something a certain way instead of being negative when the results are less than you expected.

Take a few moments now to complete the following exercise.

Exercise #8:

Improving Your Leadership Skills

- Name three things you will do to better communicate the vision of your mission or objectives to the people you lead.

  1. _____

     _____

     _____

     _____

  2. _____

     _____

     _____

     _____

  3. _____

     _____

     _____

     _____

2. Do your friends and colleagues consider you a good listener? Yes ☐   No ☐

3. Among your associates and colleagues, who is considered the best listener?

   _____

- Name at least three things this individual does that you can learn to do:

    1. _____

    _____

    2. _____

    _____

    3. _____

    _____

- Compassion not only includes consideration for others, but also may include a diplomatic and assertive ability to counsel followers when they err. Do those you answer to consider this one of your strengths? Yes ☐   No ☐

- If you answered "no," who do you know who has this strength?

    _____

- Name three things you can learn from this individual:

    1. _____

    _____

    _____

    2. _____

    _____

    _____

    3. _____

    _____

Following the Warrior

Because Warriors project confidence, they aren't difficult leaders to follow. They are strong silent types who control their emotions. They don't reveal much of themselves to anyone other than close friends and family. An icy glare greets attempts at flattery and cajolery. A growling one-liner resists attempts at solicitousness. In the workplace, these people seldom establish deep personal relationships—they don't want their objectivity clouded. Attempts to approach these leaders on a personal level before establishing a professional relationship won't work.

Objectives comprise the focus of the Warrior, and "driven" describes his or her outlook. Stay alert to the fact that this type of leader doesn't always verbalize the details necessary for achieving his or her objectives: Warriors who have learned to improve their leadership skills will go through a set procedure of verbal and written instruction, but less-experienced Warriors may assume that everyone on the team has the same focus. Don't be afraid to ask well-thought-out questions or to suggest that a mission or project be put in writing.

Time is the commodity the Warrior values most. You may have already noticed that such individuals aren't good at small talk. However, if you start a conversation with, "I have an idea that will save us time," you'll have an immediate audience. When you've completed a session with this person, it's not a good idea to linger. Thank him or her and leave.

This type of leader likes choices. When making a presentation, offer choices of good, better, or best. "Best case/worst case" scenarios work well if you're giving a situation report. Casting any report in black-and-white terms is always a safe bet with this style of leadership. The Warrior may view excessive rhetoric as camouflage, so be concise and efficient.

If you disagree with this leader, have a logical reason for the disagreement. Emotional resistance will not fly. Disagreement based on perceived inconvenience will elicit a single raised eyebrow. Present sound, rationale reasons for your point of view. Very importantly, let the Warrior know that just because you disagree with a decision doesn't mean you won't give a first-rate effort. You may have the surprise of witnessing the Warrior reverse a decision if you've presented a logical disagreement (though it might not occur to him or her to give you credit for the reversal).

It's bad communication to begin a dialogue with anyone implying their thinking is wrong, but with this type of leader, you run a *very* high risk if you do so without a logical basis. Whether you actually have facts to back this allegation or not, be prepared for storm clouds if you initiate a dialogue by implying this leader is wrong.

If you agree with the Warrior, it's best to assent simply by getting to the task at hand. Note, though, that if you agree with this leader for no other reason than to gain favor, expect to vigorously defend your position.

Warriors are well-organized people who believe that organization is a key to success. Disorganization or sloppiness will cause constant conflict with this leader. In today's workplace, many managers have been trained not to focus on anything "picayunish," so if your leader has been ignoring you lately, look around your work area—if it's cluttered, reorganize! You will probably stop the Warrior in his or her tracks and may even elicit an approving smile. If this is the person who could recommend you for a promotion, good organization on your part will definitely help your cause.

Exercise #9:
Learning From the Warrior's Style

- If the leader you follow fits the description of the Warrior, list three characteristics about this leader that you admire:

  1. _____

  _____

  2. _____

  _____

  3. _____

  _____

- Which of these characteristics do you think you have?

  _____

  _____

  _____

- List three weaknesses you think the person you follow has:

  1. _____

  _____

  2. _____

  _____

  3. _____

  _____

• Do you have some of these weaknesses? Which ones?

_____

_____

_____

• If you have listed the same weaknesses as those you think your leader has, examine the area of weakness that needs the most work and list three steps you will take to overcome it.

1. _____

_____

_____

_____

2. _____

_____

_____

_____

3. _____

_____

_____

_____

Chapter 6

The Cheerleader

Tune in any sporting event on television and watch the person stalking the sidelines and waving his or her arms around. Forget the sweater-clad students trying to build a human pyramid on the sidelines; the Cheerleader all eyes are drawn to is that excitable coach exchanging a few choice words with a game official. You feel inspired just watching. Even when seated, he or she will have an arm draped over a player's shoulder or a forefinger poking into a chest. You just know this person won't feel loved unless the team dumps the contents of an ice cooler on him or her at the game's final whistle. Recognize the signs? Take a closer look by responding to the statements in Exercise 10.

Exercise #10:
Recognizing the Cheerleader in You

	Yes	No
1. "Full steam ahead and let's get on to the next thing!" pretty much sums up my attitude towards completing a project.	☐	☐
2. I can be very emotional when I'm excited.	☐	☐
3. People have told me that if I sat on my hands, I wouldn't be able to talk.	☐	☐
4. I like a fast-moving environment with exciting people.	☐	☐
5. Regardless of how much pressure there is in the workplace, there's always time for a good story.	☐	☐
6. The more flexible and changeable my work environment, the better I like it.	☐	☐
7. I understand the need for details, but I prefer to have someone else handle those.	☐	☐
8. Sometimes people just don't understand how I feel.	☐	☐
9. I love praise for a job well done and feel dissatisfied if I don't get it.	☐	☐
10. When making decisions, I often go with my "gut feeling."	☐	☐

Seven or more "yes" answers places your leadership style in the Cheerleader category.

Personality Snapshots

Walking into the office of a Cheerleader can be a memorable experience. Trophies serve as hat racks. Pictures of this character shaking hands with any number of known and unknown people may fill one wall. The desk may be unrecognizable as a desk, with piles of papers slipping off the sides. The calendar will never be open to the correct date and will probably also serve as a repository for phone messages. It will also substitute for the Rolodex, given by a thoughtful assistant, still in its original box somewhere under the pile of papers.

If you're a visitor, the greeting is warm and effusive: "How's the family? How's life treating you?" Questions are asked sincerely and punctuated by laughter. There will always be time for interruptions. The Cheerleader accepts several phone calls amid a confusion of employees entering and reentering the office, each time apologizing with "Excuse me, I have to take this call."

When the office is quiet for a few moments and the two of you engage in conversation, you feel the warmth of someone who genuinely cares about people. The Cheerleader's body language is usually open, and he or she appears to be in constant motion. Expansive and creative use of hands and arms punctuate the conversation.

This leader appears to have no concept of time. An assistant may interrupt frequently to remind him or her of another appointment, but the Cheerleader brushes away the reminders with laughter and a wave of the hand, slipping into another story that illustrates yet another point.

You'll spend a great deal of time talking about relationships. How others "feel" about a decision and what people "think" about each other are concerns of the Cheerleader. He or she will spend time asking what you "think" or "feel" about the situation being discussed, perhaps even calling a couple of people in from the hallway with the same questions. An unscheduled meeting ensues. You'll notice that eye contact from this person is intense—Cheerleaders don't take their eyes off the person speaking.

These leaders are the most powerful at communicating the vision of their leadership. Not only can they communicate their vision clearly, they can do it inspirationally. The danger, though, is they may change their mind in midstream—their restlessness causes them to constantly tinker with good ideas.

Though the good ones in this category have integrity, a lack of concern for details can get them in trouble. Ensuing disputes over what was and wasn't promised can cast aspersions on a Cheerleader's integrity. Their compassion, however, is never in doubt, even when they're angry. The Cheerleader values human relations above all. If you're the victim of an angry tirade, you can count on the Cheerleader to come back to you later with a "pick me up." That's behavior anyone in a leadership position should be able to exercise.

Improving Leadership Skills

If you're of the Cheerleader mold, your detractors may criticize you as manipulative. You say personable. They say excitable. You say stimulating. Some may think you are undisciplined. You're convinced you're just enthusiastic. Perhaps some feel you have a tendency to overreact. You feel that you need the "dramatic" to underscore an important point. Some may view your personality as self-promotional. Others see you as gregarious. All of these characteristics are true to one degree or another.

As a leader, both your vision and your ability to communicate it are superb. You must curb, however, your tendency to change visions and create confusion in the people you lead. You need to pause when making any decision that could mean a change in the objectives you've stated. Look at the facts. Count to ten. Rewrite the game plan before announcing it to your constituency. You will benefit greatly from a written long-range plan that includes a timetable and specific objectives. (Your face may have just twisted into a painful scowl after reading this.) Few people will question your seemingly natural leadership characteristics, but developing pure management skills such as planning, organization, and time management is mandatory if you want to be a more focused leader.

Inattention to detail can create image problems for you. Too many details slipping through the cracks cast a long shadow on your credibility. Develop a good eye for detail by surrounding yourself with people who have this talent. Pay attention to them. You will learn better organization, and they will gain greater "people" skills from you.

Because you like to get people on your side of the fence, be careful of the commitments you make. "Underpromising" and "overdelivering" is a policy to consider. This policy will build trust in the people you lead. If your team sees you as prone to exaggeration, you may maintain their affection but lose their respect. The leader with less "pizzazz" but more focus may soundly defeat you in competitive situations.

Compassion is your strength because human interaction is very important to you. However, you must guard against misplaced compassion clouding your judgment. Be very wary when the people you lead bring you "tales of woe." Check the details before agreeing to favored treatment that may cause dissension in the ranks and interfere with attaining objectives.

Through the force of your personality, you have the talent to inspire loyalty in those you lead—more than any other leadership style. You must guard against team members having to "cover" for you. Sometimes in their zeal to defend an emotional comment you have made, or in covering details you did not cover, the momentum of fulfilling the mission slows. When momentum stalls, it's wise to count to ten and ask yourself what *you* need to do in planning or documentation to get things back on track. This is the time to find out "why" efforts have slowed rather than "who" is responsible.

Angry, negative tirades directed at an individual team member can adversely affect an entire team. Though things may appear to be moving thereafter, people are probably doing so without direction. A loss of focus occurs as some team members console the victim, while others may delight in the fact that they weren't the victim this time. By the time you get around to patching things up with the recipient of the "dressing down," it's almost too late. Momentum strains itself. If you're in a competitive situation, the competitor with the icy demeanor (the one you've often said has no personality) can pull ahead of you.

Be wary of people who approve of everything you do. Those who give unconditional approval are not motivated by unconditional love. Unconditional approval from a team member may later require reciprocal treatment (this may occur at the moment you need results from this individual).

Though you're very articulate, you need to resist the impulse to use this gift purely for emotional effect. Your excitement and emotion will not sway everyone in your constituency. Because logic works best with some team members, it's worth the effort to spend time building a fortress of logic for them. In doing so, you will gain their intellectual respect and approval. You may greatly benefit from having a "Human Computer" as a team member. They are great standard-bearers and quality control people as well as great planners. Having a great planner on any team you lead is a very good idea.

Better planning, organization, and double-checking yourself and team members are valuable keys to successful leadership. Though many may have characterized you as a born leader, don't forget that leadership is an art. Art requires discipline. Discipline may require you to institute policies you don't personally like. The word "paperwork" comes to mind and probably causes smoke to pour from both of your ears. Take a deep breath … count to ten … and give it some consideration. It could make you an invincible leader!

Double-check yourself now with the following exercise.

Exercise #11:
Improving Your Leadership Skills

- Have you made a recent promise in the execution of a mission or the pursuit of an objective you were unable to keep? Yes ☐   No ☐

- What was the promise?

  _____

  _____

  _____

- Name three ways this incident may have hurt the execution of the mission or slowed attainment of the objective:

  1. _____

  _____

  _____

  2. _____

  _____

  _____

  3. _____

  _____

  _____

- List three ways you can avoid overpromising and underdelivering:

  1. _____

  _____

  _____

  2. _____

  _____

  _____

  3. _____

  _____

  _____

- Do your bosses and colleagues consider you to be well-organized? Yes ☐   No ☐

- If you answered "No," list (in order of priority) three areas of your personal or professional life you can better organize:

  1. _____

  _____

  _____

  2. _____

  _____

  _____

  3. _____

  _____

  _____

Following the Cheerleader

Life is never dull following the Cheerleader. It's a roller-coaster ride compared to the point "A" to "B" bullet train of the Warrior's style. With the Cheerleader, you will have many opportunities to test your leadership qualities.

The first test may be your integrity as a future leader. Applause and approval motivate the Cheerleader more than anything else. If this is the way you choose to follow this leader, be prepared for the hostility of your colleagues. If the applause you render isn't genuine, you'll compromise your integrity and make enemies for the future, seriously imperiling your leadership opportunities to come.

Approval isn't the same as results. Seemingly within seconds after being anointed for a leadership role (or at the latest just a few moments after your hand is shaken and you're welcomed aboard), you'll be asked to produce results. Pleasing the leader with words he or she wants to hear won't substitute for getting results—at least not for very long.

If you're are not a social type of person, the Cheerleader is often an excellent teacher. He or she responds to warmth, so you want to avoid being cold or tight-lipped. This may be difficult if you're someone who has a logical and intellectual approach to life. If you're the type who values intellect above all qualities, avoid the impulse to sell Cheerleaders short. They direct their intelligence toward insight into other people, which is one of the reasons they express themselves so well. They understand what makes others tick, though they may appear to favor people who are more like them.

Understand that organizing isn't a Cheerleader's strength. If you're a good organizer, you can help this leader a great deal.

Many excellent professional relationships exist between enthusiastic leaders and team members with superior organization skills.

This type of leader emotionally electrifies any work environment. Occasionally, emotions escalate from breezy to gusty gale winds. When a tirade begins, you can exercise a couple of options. First, weather the storm, because it always passes. Second, be assertive and explain in private, after calm prevails, why this type of behavior damages your personal relationship. It's key to make this appeal on a personal basis rather than logically dissecting the encounter. The latter approach will not work.

If you share the same personality type as your leader, guard your productivity. Remember that you are accountable for your output. Two Cheerleaders engaged in a "what if" session may not be the most productive team.

Unless you share the same type of personality with this leader, you may often feel yourself in a caretaker role. Keep in mind that you will find few people as creative or motivating as the Cheerleader. The ones who learn the various disciplines of good organization are almost invincible. General George Patton presents a classic example of a well-organized Cheerleader. Even he outran his supply lines! Before becoming a sportscaster and hardware store pitchman, John Madden was one of the youngest coaches in professional sports to win championships with the Los Angeles Raiders. Although he epitomizes the Cheerleader personality, disorganized coaches do not win Super Bowls. Madden obviously learned something about organization, or how to hire organized support staff.

When providing solutions for a Cheerleader, you'll do well to focus on the people who will accomplish a mission rather than on the *things* or *reasons* that will do so. That doesn't mean you should overlook the capabilities of the people you suggest; it just means that if you use people as a focal point, you have a better chance of a fair hearing.

If you're the designated planner for the Cheerleader, you may have to fill in the details of how team members will accomplish the mission. Therefore, it's important for you to know how your "people" choices will have an impact on objectives. Give them reasons that support their dreams and vision.

Exercise #12:

Learning From the Cheerleader's Style

- If the leader you follow fits the description of the Cheerleader, list three characteristics about this person that you admire:

    1. _____

    _____

    2. _____

    _____

    3. _____

    _____

- Which of these characteristics do you think you have?

    _____

    _____

    _____

- List three weaknesses you think the person you follow may have:

    1. _____

    _____

    2. _____

    _____

    3. _____

- Do you have some of these weaknesses? Which ones?

  _____

  _____

  _____

- If you have listed the same weaknesses as those you think
  your leader has, examine the area of weakness that needs
  the most work and list three steps you will take to
  overcome it.

  1. _____

  _____

  _____

  _____

  2. _____

  _____

  _____

  _____

  3. _____

  _____

  _____

  _____

Chapter 7

The Human Computer

ne of the most interesting, memorable characters on the old *Star Trek* series was Mr. Spock. Viewers and crew members alike were drawn to him as an encyclopedia of data and information. In real life, these are the people others come to for the answers to complex organizational problems. Even in school, these analytical types become the person other students come to for help with math homework or some insight into a science project. Does this profile produce a familiar equation for you? Take a moment or two to consider the statements in Exercise #13.

Exercise #13:

Recognizing the Human Computer in You

	Yes	No
1. Facts and logic are the primary determinants of my decisions.	☐	☐
2. I sometimes delay decisions to wait for all the facts.	☐	☐
3. Logic and consistency are two of my intellectual ideals.	☐	☐
4. I prefer the planning stage of a project to the implementation stage.	☐	☐
5. Principles are more important than personal relationships.	☐	☐
6. I don't impose my ideas on others unless I'm sure the ideas will help.	☐	☐
7. There have been a few times in my life where I felt too weak to fight for a principle I believed in but too proud to give in.	☐	☐
8. Saying what I think is more important than expressing how I feel.	☐	☐
9. Some may feel that I am a procrastinator, but I believe in having every "i" dotted and every "t" crossed before offering an opinion.	☐	☐
10. I could just as well answer "maybe" to most of the preceding questions.	☐	☐

At least seven "yes" answers places you in the Human Computer style of leadership.

Personality Snapshots

As co-workers enter the Human Computer's office, they notice it's very neat and very high tech. Perhaps there's both a computer and a calculator because the latter has a paper tape. This individual may even have a pocket calculator and an electronic pocket phone book. He or she has learned to smile when people tease about the pocket protectors.

The top of the desk is polished to a high luster if it's wood. If it's glass, there are no visible fingerprints. Everything on the desk has its exact place, or the desktop is empty. There may be stacks of computer printouts in a corner or an office drawer or closet—the Human Computer doesn't want to discard them before double-checking for data that may be needed later.

Although the office furniture here is functional and neatly arranged, the Human Computer may not be as meticulous about his or her apparel and grooming because he or she values intellect more than appearances. The gravy stain on the otherwise neat blouse or shirt is of little concern. This leader seldom notices things like this, and certainly doesn't understand why anyone else would make a big fuss about something so trivial.

Those who visit the Human Computer notice that he or she isn't very expressive when speaking. With hands clasped on top of the desk, the Human Computer often doesn't meet the eyes of the other person in a conversation. This characteristic has nothing to do with credibility; it's just very difficult to look someone in the eye when you have two or three more important things going on in your mind.

As a leader, the Human Computer has both a clear vision of where to take the mission as well as the gnawing feeling that there isn't enough time to deal with all the details necessary to get things to a logical and successful conclusion. Sometimes this leader confuses the people being led with where he or she wants to lead them. Occasionally, followers become impatient with the details the Human Computer requires.

Such leaders create the impression that they are people of a few well-chosen words. Technical mishaps in a project seem to amuse them more than the mistakes of team members who cause the technical mishaps.

Integrity is the Human Computer's greatest asset. When asked questions, these individuals always try to give answers that are precise and intellectually honest, expecting the same from others too. If they don't get this in return, they may tend to avoid people they feel have been less than honest with them. High standards for quality often make Human computers the standard-bearers for any mission that involves them. They *are* quality control!

These leaders may feel uncomfortable talking to people about what they consider personal matters—what goes on outside the workplace should be private, not brought to the office. Consequently team members may think of them as uncompassionate or insensitive (though they just prefer not to verbalize their feelings and are disquieted when others do).

Human Computers may feel uncomfortable in a pure leadership role—one in which they must stand in front and take charge. It's easier for them to lead in a high-tech industry or one that requires working alone or takes advantage of their highly developed analytical skills. In the high-technology industries, research and development present the perfect environment for these leaders. Even if they're in charge of a project, they get to work with people who think and solve problems just as they do.

Those who work for Human Computers may feel they are being micromanaged because Human Computers make sure things are correct by inspecting even the smallest detail.

Improving Leadership Skills

If you recognize that you're a Human Computer, take some time to carefully consider the differences between management and leadership skills. Management skills such as planning are second nature to you. You often seek perfection in what you do. You will certainly be most comfortable in a field where you can use those highly developed analytical skills on a daily basis. If you're outside the data or high technology fields, you may want to use those analytical skills for some self-analysis. Effective leadership requires highly developed "people skills," or the intense desire to develop them.

Though high intelligence is your greatest asset as a person, it can pose your biggest obstacle as a leader. You may unwittingly expect others to be as intelligent as you are, which isn't logical. Those you lead may be more intelligent than you in other ways. For example, they may not have your ability to untangle complex data or technological problems, but they may understand more about human behavior than you do. It will be helpful for you to look at people individually, rather than hold them to the same intellectual standards you have. In the end, you may find analyzing what motivates people to perform a very exciting pursuit.

Human Computers have what some may consider a paralyzing instinct to check every detail of a project. Suffice it to say that delegation is a skill that could benefit the Human Computer. (Delegation skills are the topic of Chapter 11.) Details are important, but you may be able to develop a broader outlook on your objectives by teaching team members how to follow up on details. Strong leaders must always keep their eyes on the forest.

When you feel stress, it's usually related to the attempt to monitor every detail in a project. As part of your subconscious screams "overload," you start to retreat from making timely decisions in other areas you're responsible for. Try to delegate and you'll keep things on track and moving smoothly.

You may feel that interacting with others is imposing on them, but the people you lead perceive your lack of interaction as aloofness or standoffishness. Personal interaction is extremely important to leaders—and remember—it's difficult to lead from an office. Though it may be uncomfortable for you, make a point to wander around your area of responsibility and talk to people. Ask them what they're doing, or how they like what they're doing. If it makes you feel more comfortable, initially confine your questions to those that are work related. Listen to the answers. Look at the eyes of the person you're speaking with. Notice that the people you lead are very glad you asked the questions. In meetings, ask your team members if they need help with anything in your area of expertise. They may not always answer or request help, but keep asking!

You may have problems with decisions. Idealistically, you feel concerns about making exactly the right one. In the process of compiling data to analyze an objective, you may fall into the trap of waiting to accumulate more data, which leads to delaying or avoiding a decision that may be important to the people you lead. The perceived indecisiveness may lead team members to question your judgment and your self-confidence. If you compromise these elements, you start to lose the trust of your team members.

Perhaps one of the best ways to overcome perceived indecisiveness is to learn to set deadlines for all your objectives. Perhaps making a list of all the elements you will use to meet a deadline, coupled with a resolution not to exceed these elements, will help you. You might have a meeting with those you lead and solicit their opinions for setting a deadline. Is it realistic? What do we have to accomplish in order to make this deadline? Most importantly, set the same standards on this deadline as you would a finished project. Avoid anything that will make you delay. Before the team deadline, set another deadline for yourself—the last day you will review elements of the project or mission other than to make sure it's on track. Now stick to it.

Exercise #14:
Improving Your Leadership Skills

- Do you make the rounds of your area of responsibility, asking those you lead questions about their work?
  Yes ☐   No ☐

- If you answered "no," list three reasons why interacting with those you lead might be a good idea:

  1. _____

  _____

  _____

  _____

  2. _____

  _____

  _____

  _____

  3. _____

  _____

  _____

  _____

- Do you have difficulty meeting deadlines because you need one more piece of data or still another piece of the puzzle?
  Yes ☐   No ☐

- If you answered "yes," name three things you can do to increase your timeliness in meeting deadlines:

1. _____
   _____
   _____
   _____
   _____

2. _____
   _____
   _____
   _____
   _____

3. _____
   _____
   _____
   _____
   _____

Following the Human Computer

You can learn a great deal from the Human Computer. But if you're more assertive than individuals who follow this style of leadership, you may find yourself becoming impatient with them. If you have a Cheerleader personality, you can learn a great deal about planning and organization by observing a Human Computer. Taking this leader's eye for detail and planning ability and cutting it in half will help you become a more powerful leader.

Though Human Computers may have trouble sticking to a timetable themselves, this is a very good approach to use with them when outlining a plan. They like to see logical cause and effect. Forget any emotional displays—you'll get little response. Plan to be your most low-keyed and deadpan when approaching these leaders. When you start to feel somber as you talk to them, you're probably where you need to be. Avoid physical contact other than a brief handshake. Silent, unfavorable judgment greets loud behavior or flashy attire.

If you're a Cheerleader working for this type of leader, you've probably already guessed that you two are completely opposite in temperament and the way you accomplish objectives. The Human Computer will not respond well to an emotional presentation. If you're a Cheerleader and want to sell an idea to a Human Computer, be prepared well in advance. This is not a situation where you can use your usual élan and "wing it." Such an approach will not move this leader and will leave you very frustrated.

Flattery or cajolery is a totally useless tactic here. You will do better to save the sweet talking and coaxing for the family cat. If you disagree with a Human Computer, it's a good idea to have why you disagree written down in presentation form, devoid of emotion. A preponderance of pure logic usually wins. Stick to the facts.

When working for the Human Computer, always remember that you're dealing with someone who isn't the most gifted verbal communicator. If you make a commitment, follow through on it thoroughly. If you don't, you'll receive a low-keyed reminder of your commitment. For this leader, that's as serious as being braced up against a wall and suffering a full force "face rip." Leaders who display emotional outbursts may forget what they said shortly after they yell, but the Human Computer doesn't forget. This leader may not mention your lack of follow up again until it's time for a promotion or raise.

You will learn patience following the Human Computer if you are a Warrior personality. Your personalities are somewhat similar, except you are more assertive. The Human Computer is more "detailed oriented" than you are, and less sensitive to emotional needs than Warriors are. Stay on track when making a presentation. Try to avoid options that may beg the question, "What else have you got?" Presenting volumes of research will require more research. You have a better chance of making your point to the Human Computer with condensed research that draws logical conclusions. If you present volumes of research, you'll get a smile for your efforts, but you may never get to the point.

Exercise #15:

Learning From the Human Computer's Style

- If the leader you follow fits the description of the Human Computer, list three characteristics about this leader that you admire:

    1. _____

    _____

    2. _____

    _____

    3. _____

    _____

- Which of these characteristics do you think you have?

    _____

    _____

- List three weaknesses you think the person you follow may have:

    1. _____

    _____

    2. _____

    _____

    3. _____

    _____

- Do you have one or more of these weaknesses? Which ones?

  _____

  _____

  _____

- If you have listed the same weaknesses as those you think your leader has, examine the area of weakness that needs the most work and list three steps you will take to overcome it.

  1. _____

     _____

     _____

     _____

     _____

  2. _____

     _____

     _____

     _____

     _____

  3. _____

     _____

     _____

     _____

     _____

Chapter 8

The Lost Lamb

o social event is complete without the company of the Lost Lamb. This person values human relations more than anything else. This individual is not above sharing a few tidbits of gossip, but is also the person people gravitate to when they have personal problems and need advice. Sound familiar? Read some more and see if this leadership style applies to you.

Exercise #16:
Recognizing the Lost Lamb in You

	Yes	No
1. Being nice to people is the best way to deal with them.	☐	☐
2. I don't mind showing emotion when I'm happy or sad.	☐	☐
3. I feel very stressed out when I see conflict in the workplace.	☐	☐
4. When I make decisions, I want to spare the feelings of others as much as I can.	☐	☐
5. My ideal work environment has the details laid out for me.	☐	☐
6. I believe that people act primarily out of individual motives.	☐	☐
7. I would want to create a work environment that's friendly, where everyone is on a first-name basis.	☐	☐
8. I don't want to make decisions that are too risky.	☐	☐
9. People have told me I'm a very good listener.	☐	☐
10. In social situations, I'm just as happy to go along with whatever my friends want to do.	☐	☐

At least seven "yes" answers put you or someone you know in the Lost Lamb category.

As you pass the office of the Lost Lamb, the door is usually open, and quiet but animated conversations always seem to be in progress. The office appears cozy, as if the occupant lives rather than works there. Even in a large corporation with central decor, this office will be different. Perhaps there will be a painting on the wall that features people having a festive time in some distant European setting.

Various nooks feature family pictures. There may also be pictures of the Lost Lamb at parties and with friends at the last school reunion. If he or she has children, visitors will see an assortment of finger paintings and craft attempts. Friendliness radiates from this office. So does the attitude of "May I help you?"

When you speak with these leaders, you feel that they hang on every word. Their body language will be very open, their expression friendly. They will make intense eye contact. They'll ask many questions—about your family, your health, the weather outside. News or gossip of mutual acquaintances stirs their interest.

As the name suggests, Lost Lambs aren't people you often see in leadership roles. They usually don't feel motivated to lead and have little ambition for it when it's imposed on them. They become leaders as a result of circumstances. If you're in the business world long enough, you may, for example run into an heir of the family business. This may be a relative who has no business experience but rises to the occasion, or perhaps a son, daughter, or other relative who's pressured to assume responsibility.

You may see the Lost Lamb in social and church leadership roles. They love harmony and may be motivated to lead in an organization that promotes it.

Although the vision they have is usually someone else's, they are very capable of adding creative elements to that vision. Lost Lambs are strongly responsive to their feelings as well as to those of others. They may have strong moral and ethical feelings about life. However, they often lack the courage to act on their convictions. They may ally themselves with organizations with strong ethics but rely on others to fight the battles. They are extremely compassionate and caring people. In short, they make better followers than leaders. For the leader or individual who needs to work on his or her compassion, the Lost Lamb is a good person to have on the team. The Lost Lamb often has insight into individual motivation that others overlook.

Improving Leadership Skills

If you're a Lost Lamb, *supportive, willing,* and *dependable* may be three words you would use to describe yourself. Your critics may view things differently, though, thinking of you as ingratiating, shy, or emotional. Perhaps your friends have said, "You need to defend yourself more."

Overall, if you truly want to assume a position of leadership, you will benefit from assertiveness training. Of all the leadership types, Lost Lambs are the least assertive. Still, this may work to your advantage: you may have an easier time becoming more assertive than a Warrior or Cheerleader has becoming less aggressive.

There's a vast difference between gaining respect through an honest statement of your values and "giving in" to the feelings of others. Lost Lambs may state feelings and opinions with more tact than individuals who display other leadership styles. That in itself is a gift. With this sort of ability, why should you ever give in to the feelings of others just to make them feel good?

The key to developing leadership effectiveness is learning to reach. Set your goals and achieve them in a reasonable time frame. All leaders have to set goals to succeed, but the Lost Lamb will have to work the hardest on this area.

Learn to take risks. Although this may be a real stretch for you as a Lost Lamb, it will help you overcome fear. Understand that courage isn't the *absence* of fear—it's more a function of how you use fear. If you fear making unpopular decisions because people may dislike you, break down the fear. Most people don't like their friends just because those people agree with them. There are other attributes they like. Are you a good listener? Do you have a good sense of humor? Do you laugh at jokes? Do others think you're a warm person? Can they usually depend on you? You may have answered "yes" to every one of these questions. Why should you be afraid that people won't like you for disagreeing with them? Your personality is such that you are more likely to disagree with someone agreeably than any other type of personality.

If you base most of your decisions on emotion, take a page from the book of the Human Computer or The Warrior and learn to base your decisions more on logic. The best decisions you make will balance logic and emotion. Making a decision based solely on logic or on emotions can hurt your team. For example, a decision based on emotion alone can cause you to overlook important details that jeopardize a project or mission. You might, for example, allow too many workers to take vacation at once because they all say they need it. But as a result, the people left behind just work overtime to meet a production deadline. Making strictly logical decisions, on the other hand, often doesn't take the individual team members' capabilities into account.

The next time someone asks you what you think about something, tell that person. If a co-worker asks your opinion of where to eat, instead of saying "I'll go along with everybody else," say "I feel like pizza." It's a sure bet that someone in your group will suggest where to buy the pizza. Apply this technique to other things you do in the course of a week, and watch the positive reactions you'll begin to receive.

The following exercise will help you take a closer look at some of the aspects of the Lost Lamb style and help you see where you can strengthen your areas of weakness.

Exercise #17:
Improving My Leadership Skills

- Name three times you may have recently given in to someone else in a work situation or a personal conversation to keep the peace:

1. _____

_____

_____

2. _____

_____

_____

3. _____

_____

_____

- Did giving in on these situations create peace and harmony, or did your actions create any problems—for you or for others? If there were problems, what were they? (If you're not certain whether there were any problems, ask people affected by the decision if it had any negative effects.)

Situation #1._____

_____

_____

_____

Situation #2._____

_____

_____

_____

Situation #3._____

_____

_____

_____

- Name three ways you can project more assertiveness in dealing with others:

    1. _____

    _____

    _____

    _____

    2. _____

    _____

    _____

    _____

    3. _____

    _____

    _____

    _____

- Anticipate and list three situations in the coming week that call for you to be more assertive:

  1. _____

  _____

  _____

  _____

  2. _____

  _____

  _____

  _____

  3. _____

  _____

  _____

  _____

- Write a brief narrative for each situation you listed, stating how you plan to handle each situation more assertively, the problems you may encounter by being more assertive, and how you plan to handle problems that may arise:

  Situation 1. _____

  _____

  _____

  _____

  _____

  _____

Plan for assertiveness: _____

_____

_____

Problems: _____

_____

_____

How to handle problems: _____

_____

_____

Situation 2. _____

_____

_____

_____

_____

_____

Plan for assertiveness: _____

_____

_____

Problems: _____

_____

_____

How to handle problems: _____

_____

_____

Situation 3. _____

_____

_____

_____

_____

_____

Plan for assertiveness: _____

_____

_____

Problems: _____

_____

_____

How to handle problems: _____

_____

_____

Following the Lost Lamb

Unless you're a Lost Lamb yourself, you may find it difficult to work for this leader. If you're very ambitious and like to see relatively rapid progress, Lost Lambs may frustrate you. However, you may profit greatly from their humane and caring approach to people. They make great team members and internal leaders, as opposed to those who will pick up a flag and yell, "Follow me!" These people have an overabundance of compassion, an ingredient that is vital to sustaining a leadership effort over time.

If you are more assertive than this leader, you will need to strongly resist the impulse to try to rush decisions. Working for this type of individual will give you the opportunity to develop your own leadership skills: you can practice guiding these people instead of pushing them.

If you're a more assertive Warrior or Human Computer, the Lamb will give you an opportunity to work on your "small talk" skills. Because these people like to talk about their family and friends, it's wise to begin conversations by asking about them.

Understand that many Lost Lambs have a deep-seated hostility toward themselves because they feel angry for giving in so easily. At their worst, they can be extremely manipulative. Their placid demeanor may harbor some deep resentment for people who are more aggressive or assertive than they are.

The emotional pendulum swings the other way too. Lost Lambs can be among the most intensely loyal people you will ever meet. Being domineering or demanding is a dangerous way to interact; when they're in charge—you're apt to bring the ram out of the lamb in a hurry!

"Maybe" is almost a "yes" with the Lamb. Be very careful in offering guarantees or assurances. It's best to underpromise and overdeliver with these leaders.

Never lose sight of the fact that Lost Lambs are usually highly intelligent people who can easily see though subtle patronization. Although the Lamb is often very emotional, the one feeling they may hide is disapproval if they feel unfairly treated by peers or those they lead. Because they hide resentment and store it away, offenders may not feel the dull throbbing impact of the Lost Lamb's hostility until later.

Exercise #18:

Learning From the Lost Lamb Style

- If the leader you follow fits the description of the Lost Lamb, list three characteristics about him or her that you admire:

  1. _____

     _____

  2. _____

     _____

  3. _____

     _____

- Which of these characteristics do you think you have?

  _____

  _____

  _____

- List three weaknesses you think the person you follow has:

  1. _____

     _____

  2. _____

     _____

  3. _____

     _____

- Do you have one or more of these weaknesses? Which ones?

  _____

  _____

  _____

- If you have listed the same weaknesses as those you think your leader has, examine the area of weakness that needs the most work and list three steps you will take to overcome it.

  1. _____

     _____

     _____

     _____

  2. _____

     _____

     _____

     _____

  3. _____

     _____

     _____

     _____

Part 3

Developing Essential Leadership Skills

Chapter 9

Communication

The media referred to former president Ronald Reagan as "The Great Communicator." He took office during a period when the people of the United States needed a shot of self-esteem. That was the mission. Reagan was able to inspire people, projecting a forceful, endurable image to his constituency and the rest of the world. Certainly his acting background helped him communicate more effectively. But name any great leader without a sense of theater!

Reagan knew that the communication in powerful leadership is more than what one says. In the context of leadership, communication also includes *how* you say and do things. In other words, the costume one wears and one's actions also serve as powerful vehicles of communication. Is your voice firm with resolve? Is your posture erect and commanding? Do you make eye contact with the people you're addressing? Is your attire appropriate to the situation? Your manner of communication—both verbal and nonverbal—will determine others' perceptions of your leadership ability.

Let's take a look at each of the elements that go into your total communications package. Each of these elements "says" something about you—usually even more loudly than the message you're communicating with your words.

The Costume

Leaders make an effort to look like leaders. Every profession has a uniform, ranging from a strictly formal one such as those worn in the military and paramilitary units (e.g., a police force), where identifying insignia distinguish leaders, to the conservative business attire that executives wear.

Leaders may take great pains to maintain the appearance and insignia of their uniforms to set an example for the people they lead. In any business or profession, what you wear isn't as important as how you wear it. It's not necessary to be a fashion plate as long as you maintain an appearance that's dignified for your particular field. In almost no profession, no matter how casual, is it acceptable to look rumpled and ragged. Avoid frayed collars and cuffs. Press suits before you wear them.

Minimize accessories like jewelry. Wearing an assortment of rings can be very distracting. Well-manicured hands are an advantage. Dirty nails, extra long nails, or extreme nail styles are all distractions.

Run-down heels and scuffed leather may ruin an otherwise well-groomed appearance. Many people not only look at a person's eyes but also their shoes when they're sizing someone up. Remember that as a leader, you're always under a microscope. Many people are searching for flaws—any flaws.

If you're not in a job that requires a suit, good grooming is still important and may set you apart from the people you lead. Pressed work clothes and clean work boots often inspire clean, efficient work habits from your constituency.

Does the body fit the costume? Remember, good leaders project an image of high energy. Two hours of exercise spread over each week will do wonders for your appearance and your stamina. You will also find that a better appearance gives you more confidence. You can't help but project this confidence to the people you lead. Think about the last time you bought new clothing. Didn't it make you feel more confident? Think about how good you felt when you began an exercise program.

The Role

As noted at the beginning of this chapter, how you speak is as important as what you say. If what you say lacks conviction, those you lead will be hesitant to follow you. Try developing some of the techniques salespeople use before they make an important presentation. They rehearse—usually in front of a mirror or a video camera. Salespeople not only observe how they speak lines, they also watch their posture. They watch for distracting mannerisms. They make certain their body language is open and positive. If they are making a presentation that will require a response, they anticipate objections and formulate answers for these objections in front of the mirror or video camera.

Public speaking is a role that's important to a leader. If this is an area of weakness for you, find ways to improve this skill now. Ask a trusted friend or colleague who has those skills to coach you, or find out if there are any public speaking courses.

The Stage

Where you communicate is as important as what you say. You're in charge, so you have some control over the stage. As a general rule, you should communicate important messages in an area with the least number of distractions. A formal meeting room is an ideal place for getting your messages across. Take a few minutes before the meeting to prepare the room. You may have to clean up from a previous meeting—you don't want your group distracted by the notes someone else left on a blackboard.

If you don't have a meeting room, designate a particular area of the office for delivering your important communications. Find an area as free from distractions as possible, and then make an effort to reduce any distractions that do exist.

If you regularly meet in your own office, be sure to keep it neat. Your office shouldn't be a distraction to those you're communicating with. A messy office may be a small matter to you, but when you're looking for every edge you can gain, it's something to consider. If the stack of papers sliding off the corner of your desk distracts your listeners, they won't focus on what you say to them.

The Script

Regardless of what type of leadership role you have, written communication is also important. You'll often be required to write memos, letters, and reports. Remember that besides the people you lead, you're probably accountable to someone else too. In a supervisory or leadership capacity, it's often not enough to relay information to your own supervisor verbally.

Generally, a written document should support policy, instruction, or changes. A written document minimizes misunderstandings. It gives you a platform for answering questions. For example, let's say you have a change in policy in your department. It's important. You schedule a meeting to discuss the change. You announce the change at the meeting. You explain the change and the ramifications. You solicit questions. You may then distribute the memo and ask your team members to read the memo. You again solicit questions. At this point, there should be few individuals who don't understand the change in policy. Even with a formal procedure such as this in place, you'll still have to follow up with some team members. Face it—repetition is an integral part of leadership.

Exercise #19:
How Well Do You Communicate?

The following statements will help you determine how you communicate your message of leadership to your followers. If you aren't sure of an answer, get some feedback from a close friend or spouse. Items that you score below a "5" are communication weak links. Answers above "7" are your strengths. Challenge yourself to find ways to make your links stronger.

Disagree   Agree

1. As a matter of personal pride, I take special care of my clothing and grooming.

   1 2 3 4 5 6 7 8 9 10

2. My posture and carriage are erect and forceful.

   1 2 3 4 5 6 7 8 9 10

3. I make good eye contact with the people I talk to.

   1 2 3 4 5 6 7 8 9 10

4. I enjoy public speaking, and my friends think I'm a good storyteller.

   1 2 3 4 5 6 7 8 9 10

5. When I have an important statement to make, I write it out first.

   1 2 3 4 5 6 7 8 9 10

6. When I write out my statement or speech, I try to anticipate questions or answers from my audience.

1 2 3 4 5 6 7 8 9 10

7. I keep my work area neat and clean as an example to my co-workers.

1 2 3 4 5 6 7 8 9 10

8. When I schedule a meeting, I'm the first one to arrive at the meeting area so I can take care of last-minute details.

1 2 3 4 5 6 7 8 9 10

9. I constantly look for different ways to get my message across to my constituents in a positive fashion.

1 2 3 4 5 6 7 8 9 10

10. I always make certain that those I communicate with understand exactly what I want to get across.

1 2 3 4 5 6 7 8 9 10

Chapter 10

Motivation

owerful motivation encourages followers to "Take this job and love it!" Great leaders are always great motivators, able to inject a sense of mission and urgency in the people they lead. In other words, they are powerful communicators of their *vision*. Their *integrity* gives their followers focus. Their *compassion* shows their interest in the people who follow them. In short, VIC is extremely active in the motivation process.

The challenge of motivation lies in keeping followers alert and interested in the mission or objective—and effective leaders may find different ways of doing this. Monetary incentives, free time, recognition, and advancements are all standard in many organizations, for example. In organizations where some or all of these are not standard, the leader's challenge is even greater.

Balance in awarding any incentive or privilege is very important. Followers may ignore praise that is offered too often. People may come to expect incentives that are offered too readily. Team members who ask "What's in it for me?" rather than stating "I love my job!" aren't well motivated. How would *your* followers respond?

The physical and emotional environment can contribute equally to the motivation process. Motivation is much like the construction of a play—the cast of characters, their interaction, the plot, the stage, the props, and the theater all play a significant part. The director of the play, or leader, hires and rehearses the cast, designs the set, rehearses, designs the props, rehearses, and rehearses. Of course the director also will usually be implementing someone else's script, have little control over the budget, and have no say about the location of the theater. He or she may negotiate with the investors on how much money to spend on advertising and promotion. When a disgruntled star goes to a producer or investor, the director has to deal with that too!

The Cast

Motivation always begins with people. Most importantly, motivation begins with the *right* people for the mission or objective. If you're in a new leadership situation, assessing and knowing your followers is a priority. Even a tenured leader must constantly check that he or she has the right staff in the right positions. Make a list of your mission objectives and a list of your team's personality traits and skills. Do they match?

Though leaders might like to think that enthusiasm will carry team members through any mission, enthusiasm often isn't enough. Enthusiastic salespeople hired to accomplish an accounting mission would probably miss the mark. Though that's an extreme example, its purpose is to emphasize the need for care in positioning the right people for the job. This requires knowing your team and what motivates them individually. Although unsuitable team members obviously can negatively influence a mission, you can't discard resources without careful consideration. An actor who does comedy occasionally auditions for a drama. Many directors would have a natural inclination to dismiss the comedian without further thought. However, the wise leader, knowing that talent is talent, may use the brightness of the comedian to contrast tragedy in the drama.

In the process of motivation, a small team is hardly different from a company or a large division; the level is just more intimate and requires more coaching skills. Leading a large division may demand that you interact daily with specialists who run smaller components of the division. The specialists may parallel the skills of a small team. There may be technical, financial, promotional, sales, and marketing specialists in the large division or small company; a team may have a hand in all of these functions. If these were stage productions, we might see a contrast between the simplicity of a one-act play and the extravagance of a Broadway musical.

There are two methods of direct motivation. The first occurs on a group level; the second on an individual one. Both levels, however, require positive reinforcement when people do a good job. This may take the form of public and private praise, awards, or incentives of various types.

At the group level, leaders train group members and discuss progress through formal communication methods. That is, the leader may solicit opinions, conduct brainstorming sessions, or excite the team to higher levels of achievement. In short, group motivation requires *meetings.*

Most people don't like meetings! Many leaders like them less than their followers and consequently don't schedule them. Some leaders like them so much they'll schedule meetings that last an entire day. The best policy is to schedule as few meetings as possible each week and avoid allowing a single meeting to last more than an hour. Announce exceptions to this policy in advance. Let followers know how long you expect the change to remain in place. For example, "We will have three meetings a week until we pass this crisis."

Avoid scheduling meetings when attention levels may be low. Monday morning and Friday afternoons are two good examples of bad timing for meetings—neither promotes good concentration. On Monday morning, followers are still in weekend mode. On Friday, their minds are on the upcoming weekend. Many followers actually would perceive such scheduling as punishment. The one who really gets punished is the leader, who throughout the week has to continually say, "Didn't we cover this in Friday's (or Monday's) meeting?"

At the individual level, direct motivation is both more intense and more delicate. The leader must show a degree of individual interest without becoming familiar. The Warrior leader may have the best policy in this regard: "Establish personal relations only after establishing professional relations." Individual direct motivation often takes the form of personal coaching. A good leader will keep key followers at the same level of comprehension, but doing so may entail individual coaching in time management or organization.

One of the most powerful ways a leader can motivate is to ask the opinions of followers on matters related to the mission. "What would you do in my place? What do you see that I might not see?" Ask them about their professional goals and objectives. Look for ways to help them arrive at these goals and objectives. One of the great opportunities a leader has for learning is from team members who have different approaches to problem solving. Maintaining a high level of interest in what your followers are about goes a long way toward maintaining a high level of interest in the mission and the objectives.

Follow up all group meetings and important individual meetings in writing. Make sure followers understand what you're telling them. Written follow-up presents leaders with a valuable chronology of events for future planning as well as a tool for periodic situation reviews.

The Stage

The physical and emotional environment you create influences how your cast plays their roles. Just as a play may require chalk marks on the stage to determine position of the characters, followers need direction. The very first step in setting the stage is helping team members understand the mission. Those who understand it are better performers. It's difficult to perform as a virtuoso while scratching your head.

In spite of all that's written about "mission statements," many organizations forget or avoid this very basic form of communication. A mission statement defines a bare stage. It gives all players their purpose, understanding, and direction, plus a foundation for making decisions. A mission statement should be concise, but it must be more than a slogan to accomplish anything. "To protect and serve" could be just a slogan for a police department unless expanded. "To protect and serve the people of Anywhere, USA" directs leaders or followers in a police department to ask whom they are serving or protecting when they make a decision that could imperil the welfare of others.

Objectives differ from missions in their specificity. Objectives are defined by quantitative values, like time and money. Each follower should have a clear picture of short-, mid-, and long-range goals. Objectives should be reasonable, with follower input. If a follower can't accomplish an objective, it's the leader's responsibility to find out why. Questions like "What (or who) do you need to accomplish an objective?" are crucial to setting the stage.

Good working conditions also play an important part in stage setting. Consider everything from the lighting to the lunchroom. How does your work environment compare with that of your followers? Is yours too opulent? Is theirs cramped? A strong leader faces the same elements as his or her followers. Providing a cramped emotional or physical environment not only brings followers closer together, it also gives them a better opportunity to plan a mutiny!

The Props

Having the proper tools to do the job is an extremely important aspect of motivation. If you're in an industrial environment where safety is a consideration, team members won't work effectively if they fear for their safety. Very bad environments produce very high absence rates as well as compromised output. An informed, observant leader always knows the minimum quality and quantity of tools needed for a good performance, as well as the extras that will make followers whistle while they work.

Rehearsal

The best plays are the best rehearsed. The most successful sports teams are the ones that thoroughly practice executing the basics. Within the cycles of the workplace, training builds confidence, confidence breeds success, and success creates greater confidence. Positive training creates a positive attitude that in turn creates momentum. Momentum heightens morale.

Training should be mission-specific. If you lead salespeople who sell advertising, you train them in other media as well as your own. Train widget salespeople in every aspect of widgets from history to production. Teach them to plan their individual efforts in such a manner that your company dominates the widget market.

Just as the lead role in a play has an understudy, one of your followers should be your understudy. Train someone to assume leadership in your absence. On a small team, rotate the responsibility among all team members. Cross-training is common in elite military combat units. In the Army, for example, Special Force A-team members may be cross-trained in specialties such as demolitions or communications. If a mission is demolitions- or communications-specific, any team member with that specialty may lead the mission, regardless of rank. Cross-training also breaks up monotony and gives teams, groups, and individuals a better understanding of the "big picture."

Inspirational training usually has short-term effects. A guest speaker who can charge up a team and reinforce the leader's message in a different style provides motivating reinforcement of your mission purposes. Some team members will respond to inspirational tapes; some to multimedia presentations that include audiotape, text, and video. Specific skills like accounting may be the only ones of interest to certain team members. As the leader, you must be able to steer your staff in the right direction even when the training medium is not one of your favorites. New leaders often make a mistake by offering the same training solutions to all their followers.

A strong leader assesses group and individual training requirements and develops appropriate training programs accordingly. Post group training plans quarterly. Always solicit mission-specific training requirements directly from your constituency. Asking them for a training "wish list" is a great way to uncover training deficiencies.

Sit down with your constituents on an individual basis and discuss a personal and/or professional development program. Find out what their needs are. Help them set up the program with reasonable goals if they aren't already goal oriented. Let them pursue it independently if that's their style. Examples of such programs may include everything from physical fitness for increased energy to assertiveness training for more docile team members.

The Theater

Actors have to know where the squeaky boards are on the stage. They have to know how a theater's lighting reflects on them. They have to know how close to the stage the front-row seats are. Professional actors must know this information for any number of theaters, especially if a show goes on the road.

If you have missions and objectives that compete with someone else's, you have to supply your followers with a positive but realistic flow of information. A constituency that fears its competition won't perform well. Leaders who rely on vision can't manage with their heads in the sand; pretending things are all right when they aren't fools no one. In competitive situations, strong leaders look for ways to exploit the weaknesses of their competitors. They search for and develop niches previously overlooked. Very importantly, they seek the counsel of their front-line people. In short, leaders become strong and knowledgeable enough to direct their play in any theater in the country to a standing ovation.

The next exercise is worded in such a way that you can also ask team members to complete it as a means of capturing their feedback. After analyzing and arranging the results, schedule a meeting and discuss how you can make positive changes together.

Exercise #20:

Are You Using Your Leadership Ability to Motivate Your Followers?

The following items contribute to motivation in the workplace. For each item, first respond to the statement on the scale of 1 to 10. Then list at least one significant contribution you could make to improve this area.

1. I know and understand the mission of my organization.

Strongly Agree   Strongly Disagree

1 2 3 4 5 6 7 8 9 10

What can I do to improve my understanding of the organization's mission?

_____

_____

_____

_____

_____

_____

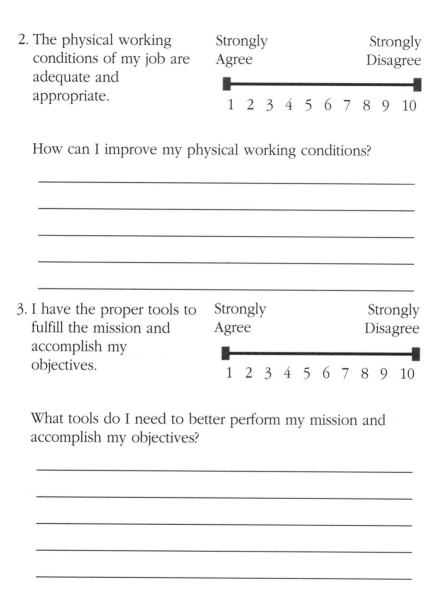

2. The physical working conditions of my job are adequate and appropriate.

Strongly Agree   Strongly Disagree

1 2 3 4 5 6 7 8 9 10

How can I improve my physical working conditions?

_____

_____

_____

_____

_____

3. I have the proper tools to fulfill the mission and accomplish my objectives.

Strongly Agree   Strongly Disagree

1 2 3 4 5 6 7 8 9 10

What tools do I need to better perform my mission and accomplish my objectives?

_____

_____

_____

_____

_____

4. I have received adequate training to accomplish my mission.

Strongly Agree   Strongly Disagree

1 2 3 4 5 6 7 8 9 10

What training or personal development programs would improve my performance?

_____

_____

_____

_____

_____

5. Do I give (receive) necessary individual time to the people I lead (from the leader I follow)?

Strongly Agree   Strongly Disagree

1 2 3 4 5 6 7 8 9 10

What can be done to improve this area?

_____

_____

_____

_____

Chapter 11

Delegation

Before kids had training wheels on bicycles, parents performed the tasks of guidance and support. Mom or Dad balanced the bike and guided it up and down the sidewalk while you adjusted your weight from side to side. Maybe, if your feet didn't reach the pedals, you even had some pedal blocks fashioned from odd wood scraps. You gradually learned to coordinate the balance of the operation, turning the pedals and steering with parental encouragement in your ear. Soon Mom's or Dad's hand just rested on the seat. As your skill increased, you less and less frequently looked over your shoulder.

That's delegation—being human training wheels!

As a parent, it's not long before you start the process all over when junior learns to drive. That's the outcome of delegation—

giving people more responsibility and more authority so they can grow. The fruits of strong delegation are always increased output and efficiency. Risk taking is healthy for both leader and follower, enabling all involved to stretch and grow.

Delegating effectively exerts a positive influence on a leader's vision, integrity, and compassion, but not delegating—or delegating improperly—can have disastrous effects. When leaders become bogged down in details, they may allow the forest to burn while they're remeasuring the girth of a tree. Their vision becomes confused. The burden of details also delays decisions and fosters an image of indecisiveness, which followers perceive as weakness. Very importantly, failure to delegate authority also demonstrates a lack of compassion. It tells a team member, "I don't trust you" and "You'll never be able to do the job as well as I can." Compassionate leaders build trust in their constituency.

Managers are sometimes afraid to make mistakes and afraid for subordinates to make mistakes that could reflect badly on their management. A manager may attempt to cover fear of delegation with statements like "It's quicker for me to do it myself" or "The job is too complex to teach someone else." Plain and simple, not delegating shows fear. Worse, the fear may give way to peevishness and anger over the prison created by masses of paperwork, overwork, and delayed decisions. That anger eventually will erupt, creating greater setbacks in motivation, morale, and achievement of mission objectives.

Delegation should be an act that promotes individual growth. Think about the first time one of your parents handed you the car keys. Were you proud? Did you think about the new world being opened to you? Initially your parents probably restricted your driving to the neighborhood, but as you gained their trust, and showed growth in other areas, your driving radius no doubt widened proportionately.

What would have happened, though, if you had taken driver's education, spent time with a parent behind the wheel, demonstrated responsibility in all facets of your life, and yet never saw those car keys? You still washed the car every week, but drive it? "Nope! you're not ready yet!" How would that have made you feel? That's how your followers may react if they're never allowed to steer for part of the journey.

Real delegation can be a powerful motivator. Real delegation offers solid training opportunities. Real delegation prepares team members for greater responsibility. Therefore, real delegation does not mean just tossing followers the things you don't want to do yourself. In order to be beneficial, delegation must include a duty, give a person authority, and require an obligation. Let's look at a sales operation or organization as a typical example of delegation, as a sales department is one area of a company that cannot survive without dividing up the pie.

Salespeople prepare proposals, make appointments, call on accounts, and make sales. One person cannot do all this and keep an enterprise afloat—these are duties that several salespeople perform within territories or categories of accounts. In many organizations, a vast army of salespeople takes to the streets each day, the theory being "the more salespeople, the more sales."

Salespeople usually have authority to price their product within certain limits. This is more true when selling intangibles like advertising as opposed to tangibles like copy machines. The fact remains that unless managers give salespeople some pricing authority, sales momentum sputters. If the sales manager reserves the authority to approve everything, the sales representative usually has to make one or more phone calls to the manager or set up an extra appointment with the client. This can guarantee a lost sale. True delegation in this situation dictates that the sales manager merely checks each contract to make certain the prices and specifications fall within the limits of the company's pricing policy. The extension of authority eliminates bottlenecks.

In addition, salespeople have an obligation to perform to certain standards. Most organizations, for example, require a certain number of calls per week, and sales staff must generate a certain percentage of sales from these calls. They agree with management on goals by month, quarter, and year. Both parties know what these obligations are and meet regularly to discuss progress and difficulties.

Sales departments clearly answer the three mandatory questions in the delegation process:

- What is the duty that I am delegating?

- What authority am I relinquishing and giving to the delegate?

- What responsibility will the delegate have for contributing to the mission or objective?

Delegating in a sales operation obviously is almost mandatory—a leader in this arena who does not delegate effectively will not endure. Perhaps, though, you're a leader in an administrative area, or the owner and president of your company. Does that change the playing field? No—you should delegate regardless of who you lead, and you should ask the same three questions.

The first step in developing a delegation program involves taking an honest look at yourself and assessing how you want to grow. A major trap in leadership is failing to set aside time for personal growth. This oversight eventually taps out your reservoir of new experience to share with your constituency. Delegation does two things for leaders: it helps you to develop your "people" skills, and once you complete the delegate training process, you'll have more time for your own individual and professional growth. In short, it's going to get you back up in that fire tower so you can look at the entire forest.

The next step is an assessment or reassessment of your mission or objectives. Make a list of the key elements you need for either mission or objective, such as administration, meetings, supervision, training, and so forth. How much time are you spending in each area? Is this productive time for you? Where could you be spending more time to accomplish your mission or objective?

Next, make a list of everyone (or just the key people) you lead and match their capabilities with your list of key elements. Do you need to talk to them about their professional goals? How can delegation help fulfill these goals? This is a great time to make a list of what you think your followers need for personal or professional growth.

For example, maybe you're spending too much time in administration. Is it necessary for you to review every piece of paper that comes across your desk? Channel some to a team member and tell him or her what you want. Ask for opinions after he or she has reviewed the material. Is research a part of your responsibility? Give some to an able assistant who may only be typing (and languishing in the process).

Delegation not only helps you cover existing ground—it can allow your team to explore new territory. For instance, "Our followers need better training!" seems to be a universal cry of leaders. Training seminars are perfect for most needs, but what do you do internally? When you assess the strengths of your followers, you'll get a picture of the skills they have. Set up in-house training that features these individual skills. Make each follower responsible for a training session that includes information and handouts.

Just remember when you delegate that it's the same as giving someone the keys to your car. Whether that's a BMW or an old Ford Pinto, there are obligations and responsibilities that accompany the keys. Cover these thoroughly, including a discussion of what this delegation will do for the individual. Reaffirm the trust and confidence you have in the delegate. Help set deadlines and periodically monitor results without stifling the team member(s) involved.

Before leaving this topic, there's another type of delegation that leaders come across—"upward delegation." This variety is announced loudly by the follower who breathlessly says, "Boy, oh boy! YOU have a problem!" In its lesser form, an overture from a team member begins with "I can't ..." or "I'm having a problem with ... ." or "Can you solve something for me?"

Many leaders, in a misplaced sense of feeling useful, twist themselves into all sorts of mental and physical contortions to solve the problem. One simple question, however, will prevent upward delegation. Ask your follower, "How do you think we should solve this problem?" Then sit back and wait for an answer. Usually he or she will have a solution, or at least something close that will create less strain for you. If not, gently dismiss him or her until a solution materializes. Say, "You pose an interesting dilemma. Why don't you get back to me this time tomorrow with a list of things that will help solve the problem?"

Complete the exercise on the next page to help you explore your delegation options.

Exercise #21:
Assessing Your Delegation Possibilities

- What areas within my current mission do I need to devote more time to in order to be a more effective and efficient leader?

  _____

  _____

  _____

  _____

  _____

  _____

  _____

- What factors prevent me from spending time in these areas?

  _____

  _____

  _____

  _____

  _____

  _____

- How can I delegate these tasks to other team members without judging their capability or training?

  _____

  _____

  _____

  _____

- Looking at my best-case option, what will I delegate to the individual or individuals in the areas of task, authority, and responsibility?

  Task: _____

  Authority: _____

  _____

  Responsibility: _____

  _____

- Looking at the best-case option, what training or development will I have to give the individual(s)?

  _____

  _____

  _____

  _____

- What will be the objective of the training?

  _____

  _____

  _____

- What is the time frame I need to administer this training?

  _____

  _____

  _____

- What is a reasonable timetable for the delegate to complete the delegation, from beginning to end, that will also allow time for discussion with the delegate?

  _____

  _____

  _____

  _____

- When the delegation process is completed, how many hours per week will I save for my devotion to other priorities?

  _____

  Is this enough time? Yes ☐   No ☐

- Using the same process, what other areas can I delegate?

  _____

  _____

  _____

  _____

  _____

Chapter 12

Selling Your Leadership

ll great leaders are great salespeople, and no question better defines leadership than, "Yeah ... but would you buy a used car from this person?" Leaders have to be great salespeople to convince a constituency that the mission is worthy and the objectives are attainable. In fact, leaders have to be great salespeople to *develop* a constituency, and this happens by selling and reinforcing your beliefs every day in one way or another.

Presidential candidates and other aspirants to elected office provide ready examples of good and bad salespeople. They have to persuade a political party and a little over half the voters to buy their leadership package. Re-election then is the same as a sales renewal. Great leaders in the private sector may have to sell their vision of corporate growth to an entrenched board of directors. The head of a corporate division has to sell the financial people on funding for a major project that will contribute to a company's growth. A leader may have to sell his spouse or family on the sacrifices that leadership requires to maintain an upscale lifestyle.

Reading the words "selling" or "sales" may provoke an urge to walk down the hall to the lavatory and wash your hands. Many people's image of a salesperson is someone in a plaid suit with tired, shifty eyes, and a rapid, "mock sincere" line of chatter. Listening, however, plays a far more important role in the sales process than talking ever will.

A salesperson, like a leader, has to gain as much information from a prospect as possible. Often this means hours of asking questions and absorbing answers. It may mean days of research into the opinions and ideas of others. Then it's back to the prospect or constituency with questions that begin "What do you like about ..." "How do we...?" or "What if we ...?" Then the leader or salesperson puts all this information together in a logical sequence that will convince a constituency or a prospect that the mission is exciting and worthwhile, that the objective is attainable and extremely rewarding.

In sales, one may hear the term "selling a package deal." Vision, integrity, and compassion make up the package a leader must sell every day. There will be days when you have to sell this package to yourself as well as to your followers and those you answer to. Great salespeople and great leaders are always finding new ways to improve the "package" by asking themselves questions like:

- Is my vision clear to my followers?

- Will I compromise my integrity if I do this?

- Do I show compassion for the viewpoints and personalities of others?

If you're not sincere in the package you present, your followers will sense it quickly. Similarly, if you believe in what you're doing, you will reflect it as well.

Powerful leaders and legendary salespeople project trust and confidence. They acknowledge their fears but avoid showing them. Not showing fear is quite different from being insincere. Not showing fear or pain is an act of compassion and a source of strength for your followers. "Why get them upset?" goes the thinking. It's the ultimate act of confidence in your leadership package.

One of the greatest examples of confidence and courage came from Franklin Delano Roosevelt. Unable to walk because of polio, he would use a cane and the arm of one of his children when he set forth in public. Heavy leg braces permitted him to painfully shift his weight from one side to the other and give the appearance he was walking. This was agonizing for him. Sweat would drench him. The pressure of Roosevelt's grip bruised the arm of his human crutch. He could not allow his followers to see him less than fully standing, a position he felt was necessary for projecting confidence and courage. If he fell, he joked to ease the embarrassment of those around him. In short, he used what he had to prevent his followers from being fearful. At his inaugural address in 1933, when Roosevelt stated that "the only thing we have to fear is fear itself," he was speaking from the core of his conviction.

Like great salespeople the world over, Roosevelt was also able to focus attention away from the physical weakness of his package. He was like a vintage Mercedes, so captivating that his followers never saw the dents. Few people during his tenure as president may have been totally aware that he spent most of his time in a wheelchair. He focused the attention of his constituency on the power of his upper body. To emphasize this power, photographers framed him closely when they snapped pictures. The trademark cape served the purpose a topcoat could not to a man in a wheelchair. The unique pince nez glasses, cigarette holder, and crushed fedora focused even more of his onlookers' attention.

Influential leaders know people. Because they ask themselves many hard questions, they have a better understanding of how others feel. Great salespeople all have this trait too—they call it empathy. Leaders have a knack of putting themselves in your shoes. They know when you're wearing loafers and when you have your boot laces through all the eyelets. Leaders spend much time learning what motivates people and how different people think. Great salespeople think the same way. Selling provides a service, and so does leadership. The more you know about the people you lead, the better you will lead them. The same applies to competitors. The more you know about them, the greater will be your lead over them.

In sales, negotiation also is always part of the process of meeting the goal and getting what you want. Leaders negotiate performance with their followers to fulfill their vision. They negotiate ways and means of getting the mission accomplished with higher-ups for the same reason. They may negotiate terms with vendors and clients to improve a mission's bottom line.

Leaders should be honest in their negotiations with followers, bosses, vendors, and clients. A leader has a lot more to lose by abandoning ethical behavior in negotiations. Word spreads. Vendors and clients ask for more detail in their contractual arrangements. Management usually doesn't keep people it can't trust. Followers flee, or at least look for ways around unethical behavior.

Leaders are compassionate in their negotiations. They plan a negotiating strategy just as they would plan a sales strategy. The objective for compassionate leaders is for all parties involved in the negotiation process to win equally. Compassionate leaders always leave a door open for the opposite party in a negotiation situation. This gives the opposite party the opportunity to give ground gracefully and eliminates animosity or bitter feelings.

Selling and negotiating both require planning. Planning is the first and most important part of achieving an objective or making a sale. Whether you're presenting a new program to team members or a funding request to upper management, the plan should always take the form of a written proposal that defines the mission, states the objectives, and outlines a plan with a timetable. The timetable is important for establishing and/or negotiating deadlines. When you present the proposal to your superiors, include anticipated obstacles and solutions. If it's a project that requires salaried staff, increased resources/ supplies, and different logistics, the proposal should naturally include anticipated costs as well as profitability and benefits. In a more detailed form, training methods, new hire requirements, promotion, or advertising may be included.

Let's take a closer look:

- **Mission.** Statement of mission should be simple and used as a basis for making all decisions. Discard any thought or idea that does not fit. A mission statement might be something like "To become the fashion sales leader with the X Generation" (your focus then would be companies like Banana Republic, not Sans a Belt Slacks). What you want is a simple statement that helps you make "yes" or "no" decisions.

- **Objectives.** You may have several objectives, and if so, they may require separate proposals. Here's where you start to think about what the mission is going to cost or what it needs to gain. Objectives should be quantifiable, containing a monetary goal (sales, savings, etc.) and perhaps a percentage goal ("We will maintain a 15% sales share of the X Generation clothing market"). The objective should also be time specific ("We will obtain this objective by 1997"). Obviously if the requirements of the mission exceed the capability of the organization, you need to rethink the mission and the objective … or be prepared to do an incredible sales job.

- **Implementation**. The method of accomplishing the mission is the most detailed segment of your proposal. This is where you take the overall objective and break it down into staff hours, training, supplies/resources, and logistics. There are any number of acceptable formats for doing this. You may want to break each category down individually, for example. However you format the proposal, this is the stage where you must anticipate the areas of negotiation. In other words, what are the obstacles? What are the solutions to the obstacles? Can these obstacles be turned into benefits by removing them?

When preparing this portion of the proposal, it's wise to give careful consideration to the personality style of the person receiving the presentation. Is he or she a Warrior? (Keep it simple with "best-case/worst-case" scenarios and use bottom-line alternatives.) Human Computer? (Place emphasis on time elements.) Cheerleader? (Place emphasis on status and prestige.) Lost Lamb? (Emphasize people's needs and how they will work together.)

- **Budgeting.** How much is obtaining the objective going to cost? Veteran salespeople like to use the heading "Investment" for this area—it gets the prospect thinking there might be a return instead of merely an expenditure. The best approach is positioning investment and return concurrently. If you are a Cheerleader or Lost Lamb type, this is an important stage for you. You will have to discipline yourself to do what the Human Computer and the Warrior do naturally in this area. List all costs in the planning, right down to pencils and paper. Your organization may have a line-item budget process for annual planning. Use whatever your audience is familiar with. This is an important step to check with your team so there are no surprises.

- **Benefits.** What are the advantages to the different groups involved in the objectives? Company, division, department, employees, and consumers are all important. In stating the benefits, you should again be aware of the type of person for whom you are writing the proposal. If the benefits don't exceed the expenditures, back up and rework some of the other planning areas.

- **Summary.** Keep this section short. If you can't summarize what you have said in one hundred words or less, you might want to review the proposal. If you have a bottleneck in your proposal, you will develop bottlenecks on the way to your objective.

The following exercise will help you get any mission you undertake organized. It will enable you to spot mission pitfalls and solve them. Invite full participation when you can, letting your followers help determine the mission, objective, and elements. Try "green light" brainstorming sessions where no idea is rejected. And have some fun!

Exercise #22:
Selling Your Proposal

Mission Statement

_____

_____

Objectives

_____

_____

Implementation

Overview a chronological narrative of your vision and how it
will be implemented:

_____

_____

_____

_____

_____

_____

_____

Individual or Team

_____

_____

Objective

_____

_____

Deadline

_____

Cost

_____

Special Requirements (include costs)

Training: _____

_____

_____

_____

_____

_____

_____

Logistics: _____

_____

_____

_____

_____

_____

_____

Resources/supplies: _____

_____

_____

_____

_____

_____

_____

Advertising: _____

_____

_____

_____

_____

_____

Promotion: _____

_____

_____

_____

_____

_____

Anticipated Obstacles

_____

_____

_____

_____

_____

_____

Solutions

_____

_____

_____

_____

_____

_____

Timetable

Date _____

What's Accomplished/By Whom

_____

_____

_____

_____

_____

Investment

	Item	Cost
Personal:	_____	_____
	_____	_____
	_____	_____
	_____	_____
Logistics:	_____	_____
	_____	_____
	_____	_____
	_____	_____
Supplies/resources:	_____	_____
	_____	_____
	_____	_____
	_____	_____
Promotion:	_____	_____
	_____	_____
	_____	_____
	_____	_____
Advertising:	_____	_____
	_____	_____
	_____	_____
	_____	_____
	Total:	_____

Benefits

Profitability: _____

_____

_____

_____

_____

Goodwill: _____

_____

_____

_____

_____

What mission may accomplish for the future: _____

_____

_____

_____

_____

Overall value to the organization upon successful completion:

_____

_____

_____

_____

Bibliography & Suggested Reading

Bittel, Lester R. *Leadership: The Key to Management Success.* New York: Franklin Watts, 1984.

Covey, Stephen R. *Principle Centered Leadership.* New York: Summit Books, 1991.

Covey, Stephen R. *The Seven Habits of Highly Effective People.* New York: Simon & Schuster, 1989.

Kauzes, James, and Barry Posner. *The Leadership Challenge: How to Keep Getting Extraordinary Things Done in Organizations.* San Francisco: Jossey-Bass, 1995.

Levine, Stuart R., and Michael A. Crom. *The Leader in You: How to Win Friends, Influence People, and Succeed in a Changing World.* New York: Simon & Schuster, 1993.

Poley, Michelle Fairfield. *Mastering the Art of Communication.* Mission, KS: SkillPath Publications, 1995.

Rosenbaum, Bernard L. *How to Motivate Today's Workers: Motivational Models for Managers and Supervisors.* New York: McGraw-Hill, 1982.

Towers, Mark. *The ABC's of Empowered Teams*. Mission, KS: SkillPath Publications, 1994.

Towers, Mark. *Dynamic Delegation*. Mission, KS: SkillPath Publications, 1993.

Wills, Gary. *Certain Trumpets: The Call of Leaders*. New York: Simon & Schuster, 1994.

Available From SkillPath Publications

Self-Study Sourcebooks

Climbing the Corporate Ladder: What You Need to Know and Do to Be a Promotable Person
  by Barbara Pachter and Marjorie Brody

Coping With Supervisory Nightmares: 12 Common Nightmares of Leadership and What You
  Can Do About Them *by Michael and Deborah Singer Dobson*

Discovering Your Purpose *by Ivy Haley*

Going for the Gold: Winning the Gold Medal for Financial Independence
  by Lesley D. Bissett, CFP

The Innovative Secretary *by Marlene Caroselli, Ed.D.*

Mastering the Art of Communication: Your Keys to Developing a More Effective Personal
  Style *by Michelle Fairfield Poley*

Organized for Success! 95 Tips for Taking Control of Your Time, Your Space, and Your Life
  by Nanci McGraw

A Passion to Lead! How to Develop Your Natural Leadership Ability *by Michael Plumstead*

P.E.R.S.U.A.D.E.: Communication Strategies That Move People to Action
  by Marlene Caroselli, Ed.D.

Productivity Power: 250 Great Ideas for Being More Productive *by Jim Temme*

Promoting Yourself: 50 Ways to Increase Your Prestige, Power, and Paycheck
  by Marlene Caroselli, Ed.D.

Risk-Taking: 50 Ways to Turn Risks Into Rewards *by Marlene Caroselli, Ed.D.
  and David Harris*

Stress Control: How You Can Find Relief From Life's Daily Stress *by Steve Bell*

The Technical Writer's Guide *by Robert McGraw*

Total Quality Customer Service: How to Make It Your Way of Life *by Jim Temme*

Write It Right! A Guide for Clear and Correct Writing *by Richard Andersen and Helene Hinis*

Handbooks

The ABC's of Empowered Teams: Building Blocks for Success *by Mark Towers*

Assert Yourself! Developing Power-Packed Communication Skills to Make Your Points
  Clearly, Confidently, and Persuasively *by Lisa Contini*

Breaking the Ice: How to Improve Your On-the-Spot Communication Skills
  by Deborah Shouse

The Care and Keeping of Customers: A Treasury of Facts, Tips, and Proven Techniques for Keeping Your Customers Coming BACK! *by Roy Lantz*

Challenging Change: Five Steps for Dealing With Change *by Holly DeForest and Mary Steinberg*

Dynamic Delegation: A Manager's Guide for Active Empowerment *by Mark Towers*

Every Woman's Guide to Career Success *by Denise M. Dudley*

Great Openings and Closings: 28 Ways to Launch and Land Your Presentations With Punch, Power, and Pizazz *by Mari Pat Varga*

Hiring and Firing: What Every Manager Needs to Know *by Marlene Caroselli, Ed.D. with Laura Wyeth, Ms.Ed.*

How to Be a More Effective Group Communicator: Finding Your Role and Boosting Your Confidence in Group Situations *by Deborah Shouse*

How to Deal With Difficult People *by Paul Friedman*

Learning to Laugh at Work: The Power of Humor in the Workplace *by Robert McGraw*

Making Your Mark: How to Develop a Personal Marketing Plan for Becoming More Visible and More Appreciated at Work *by Deborah Shouse*

Meetings That Work *by Marlene Caroselli, Ed.D.*

The Mentoring Advantage: How to Help Your Career Soar to New Heights *by Pam Grout*

Minding Your Business Manners: Etiquette Tips for Presenting Yourself Professionally in Every Business Situation *by Marjorie Brody and Barbara Pachter*

Misspeller's Guide *by Joel and Ruth Schroeder*

Motivation in the Workplace: How to Motivate Workers to Peak Performance and Productivity *by Barbara Fielder*

NameTags Plus: Games You Can Play When People Don't Know What to Say *by Deborah Shouse*

Networking: How to Creatively Tap Your People Resources *by Colleen Clarke*

New & Improved! 25 Ways to Be More Creative and More Effective *by Pam Grout*

Power Write! A Practical Guide to Words That Work *by Helene Hinis*

Putting Anger to Work For You! *by Ruth and Joel Schroeder*

Reinventing Your Self: 28 Strategies for Coping With Change *by Mark Towers*

Saying "No" to Negativity: How to Manage Negativity in Yourself, Your Boss, and Your Co-Workers *by Zoie Kaye*

The Supervisor's Guide: The Everyday Guide to Coordinating People and Tasks *by Jerry Brown and Denise Dudley, Ph.D.*

Taking Charge: A Personal Guide to Managing Projects and Priorities *by Michal E. Feder*

Treasure Hunt: 10 Stepping Stones to a New and More Confident You! *by Pam Grout*

A Winning Attitude: How to Develop Your Most Important Asset! *by Michelle Fairfield Poley*

For more information, call 1-800-873-7545.

Notes

Notes

Notes

Notes